T-3
ISBN 0-8373-8003-0

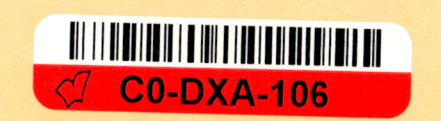

THE PASSBOOK^R SERIES

PASSBOOKS^R

FOR

TEACHERS LICENSE EXAMINATIONS

AUXILIARY TEACHER

NATIONAL LEARNING CORPORATION

20 DuPont Street   Plainview, New York 11803

516/935-5800

REF
LB
2844.1
.A8
N31

All rights reserved, including the right of reproduction in whole or in part, in any form or by any means, electronic or mechanical, including photocopying, recording, or by any information storage and retrieval system, without permission in writing from the Publisher.

Copyright © 1978 by

National Learning Corporation

212 Michael Drive, Syosset, New York 11791
(516) 921-8888

PRINTED IN THE UNITED STATES OF AMERICA

PASSBOOK SERIES®

The *PASSBOOK SERIES* has been created to prepare applicants and candidates for the ultimate academic battlefield – the examination room.

At some time in our lives, each and every one of us may be required to take an examination – for validation, matriculation, admission, qualification, registration, certification, or licensure.

Based on the assumption that every applicant or candidate has met the basic formal educational standards, has taken the required number of courses, and read the necessary texts, the *PASSBOOK SERIES* furnishes the one special preparation which may assure passing with confidence, instead of failing with insecurity. Examination questions – together with answers – are furnished as the basic vehicle for study so that the mysteries of the examination and its compounding difficulties may be eliminated or diminished by a sure method.

This book is meant to help you pass your examination provided that you qualify and are serious in your objective.

The entire field is reviewed through the huge store of content information which is succinctly presented through a provocative and challenging approach – the question-and-answer method.

A climate of success is established by furnishing the correct answers at the end of each test.

You soon learn to recognize types of questions, forms of questions, and patterns of questioning. You may even begin to anticipate expected outcomes.

You perceive that many questions are repeated or adapted so that you gain acute insights, which may enable you to score many sure points.

You learn how to confront new questions, or types of questions, and to attack them confidently and work out the correct answers.

You note objectives and emphases, and recognize pitfalls and dangers, so that you may make positive educational adjustments.

Moreover, you are kept fully informed in relation to new concepts, methods, practices, and directions in the field.

You discover that you are actually taking the examination all the time: you are preparing for the examination by "taking" an examination, not by reading extraneous and/or supererogatory textbooks.

In short, this PASSBOOK, used directedly, should be an important factor in helping you to pass your test.

EXAMINATION SECTION

CONTENTS

TEST 1

    KEY (CORRECT ANSWERS)

TEST 2

    KEY (CORRECT ANSWERS)

TEST 3

    KEY (CORRECT ANSWERS)

EXAMINATION SECTION

CONTENTS

TEST 1

    KEY (CORRECT ANSWERS)

TEST 2

    KEY (CORRECT ANSWERS)

BASIC PRINCIPLES AND PRACTICES IN EDUCATION
THE NEW PROGRAM OF EDUCATION

CONTENTS

	Page
I. PHILOSOPHY AND OBJECTIVES	1
A. Philosophy	1
B. Concepts of Education	1
C. Objectives	1
D. Methods of Achieving These Objectives	2
E. Organismic Psychology	2
F. Underlying Tenets of the Program	2
G. What Does the New Program Mean?	3
H. Advantages and Disadvantages	3
I. Traditional vs. Progressive Education	4
J. General Principles in Any Modern Philosophy of Elementary Education	4
II. THE CURRICULUM	5
A. Definitions	5
B. General Considerations	5
C. Conditions that Compel Curricular Changes	6
D. Changes that Result From Curriculum Improvement	6
E. Main Problems in Curriculum Development	6
F. Factors Affecting Curriculum Programs	7
G. Considerations for Curriculum Programs	7
H. Questions Related to Curriculum Development	7
III. GROUPING AND COMMITTEE WORK	8
A. Organizing Groups for Instruction	8
B. Criteria for Group Work	8
C. Committee Work	9
IV. EVALUATION	9
A. Items to be Evaluated	9
B. Reasons for Evaluating	10
C. Who Evaluates?	10
D. Evaluation in a Unit of Work	10
V. DISCIPLINE	12
A. Meaning	12
B. Discipline vs. Order	12
C. The Difference Between Conduct and Behavior	12

	Page
V. DISCIPLINE (cont'd)	12
D. Planes of Discipline	12
E. General Principles of Classroom Discipline	13
F. Positive vs. Negative Discipline	13
G. Why Some Teachers Have Disciplinary Troubles	13
H. Class Morale as a Factor in Classroom Discipline	13
I. The Use of Incentives	14
J. Classroom Punishments	15
K. Some Practical Suggestions for Teachers (Characteristic of Transition from Order to Discipline)	17
VI. BASIC FUNDAMENTALS OF EDUCATIONAL PSYCHOLOGY	17
A. Conditioning	17
B. Learning by Trial and Error (Connectionism)	18
C. Learning by Insight: Gestalt Psychology	18
D. The Field Theory (Organismic, Holistic Theory)	18
E. Transfer of Training	19
F. Habit	20
G. Individual Differences	21
VII. HISTORY OF EDUCATION	21
A. Leaders	21
1. Socrates	21
2. Plato	22
3. Aristotle	22
4. Comenius	22
5. Locke	22
6. Rousseau	22
7. Basedow	23
8. Pestalozzi	23
9. Herbart	23
10. Froebel	23
11. Spencer	23
12. Mann	23
13. Barnard	24
14. Dewey	24
B. Conceptualized Definitions and Aims of Education	24

HOW TO TAKE A TEST

You have studied hard, long, and conscientiously.

With your official admission card in hand, and your heart pounding, you have been admitted to the examination room.

You note that there are several hundred other applicants in the examination room waiting to take the same test.

They all appear to be equally well prepared.

You know that nothing but your best effort will suffice. The "moment of truth" is at hand: you now have to demonstrate objectively, in writing, your knowledge of content and your understanding of subject matter.

You are fighting the most important battle of your life -- to pass and/or score high on an examination which will determine your career and provide the economic basis for your livelihood.

What extra, special things should you know and should you do in taking the examination?

BEFORE THE TEST

YOUR PHYSICAL CONDITION IS IMPORTANT

If you are not well, you can't do your best work on tests. If you are half asleep, you can't do your best either. Here are some tips:
1. Get about the same amount of sleep you usually get. Don't stay up all night before the test, either partying or worrying -- DON'T DO IT.
2. If you wear glasses, be sure to wear them when you go to take the test. This goes for hearing aids, too.
3. If you have any physical problems that may keep you from doing your best, be sure to tell the person giving the test. If you are sick or in poor health, you really cannot do your best on any test. You can always come back and take the test some other time.

AT THE TEST

EXAMINATION TECHNIQUES

1. Read the *general* instructions carefully. These are usually printed on the first page of the examination booklet. As a rule, these instructions refer to the timing of the examination; the fact that you should not start work until the signal and must stop work at a signal, etc. If there are any *special* instructions, such as a choice of questions to be answered, make sure that you note this instruction carefully.

2. When you are ready to start work on the examination, that is as soon as the signal has been given, read the instructions to each question booklet, underline any key words or phrases, such as *least, best, outline, describe,* and the like. In this way you will tend to answer as requested rather than discover on reviewing your paper that you *listed without describing,* that you selected the *worst* choice rather than the *best* choice, etc.

3. If the examination is of the objective or so-called multiple-choice type, that is, each question will also give a series of possible answers: A,B,C, or D, and you are called upon to select the best answer and write the letter next to that answer on your answer paper, it is advisable to start answering each question in turn. There may be anywhere from 50 to 100 such questions in the three or four hours allotted and you can see how much time would be taken if you read through all the questions before beginning to answer any. Furthermore, if you come across a question or a group of questions which you know would be difficult to answer, it would undoubtedly affect your handling of all the other questions.

4. If the examination is of the essay-type and contains but a few questions, it is a moot point as to whether you should read all the questions before starting to answer any one. Of course if you are given a choice, say five out of seven and the like, then it is essential to read all the questions so you can eliminate the two which are most difficult. If, however, you are asked to answer all the questions, there may be danger in trying to answer the easiest one first because you may find that you will spend too much time on it. The best technique is to answer the first question, then proceed to the second, etc.

5. Time your answers. Before the examination begins, write down the time it started, then add the time allowed for the examination and write down the time it must be completed, then divide the time available somewhat as follows:
   a. If 3 1/2 hours are allowed, that would be 210 minutes. If you have 80 objective-type questions, that would be an average of about 2 1/2 minutes per question. Allow yourself no more than 2 minutes per question, or a total of 160 minutes, which will permit about 50 minutes to review.
   b. If for the time allotment of 210 minutes, there are 7 essay questions to answer, that would average about 30 minutes a question. Give yourself only 25 minutes per question so that you have about 35 minutes to review.

6. The most important instruction is *to read each question* and make sure you know what is wanted. The second most important instruction is to *time yourself properly* so that you answer every question. The third most important instruction is to *answer every question*. Guess if you have to but include something for each question. Remember that you will receive no credit for a blank and will probably receive some credit if you write something in answer to an essay question. If you guess a letter, say "B" for a multiple-choice question, you may have guessed right. If you leave a blank as the answer to a multiple-choice question, the examiners may respect your feelings but it will not add a point to your score.
7. Suggestions
   a. Objective-Type Questions
      (1) Examine the question booklet for proper sequence of pages and questions.
      (2) Read all instructions carefully.
      (3) Skip any question which seems too difficult; return to it after all other questions have been answered.
      (4) Apportion your time properly; do not spend too much time on any single question or group of questions.
      (5) Note and underline key words -- *all, most, fewest, least, best, worst, same, opposite*.
      (6) Pay particular attention to negatives.
      (7) Note unusual option, e.g., unduly long, short, complex, different or similar in content to the body of the question.
      (8) Observe the use of "hedging" words - *probably, may, most likely, etc.*
      (9) Make sure that your answer is put next to the same number as the question.
      10) Do not second guess unless you have good reason to believe the second answer is definitely more correct.
      (11) Cross out original answer if you decide another answer is more accurate; do not erase.
      (12) Answer all questions; guess unless instructed otherwise.
      (13) Leave time for review.

   b. Essay-Type Questions
      (1) Read each question carefully.
      (2) Determine exactly what is wanted. Underline key words or phrases.
      (3) Decide on outline or paragraph answer.
      (4) Include many different points and elements unless asked to develop any one or two points or elements.
      (5) Show impartiality by giving pros and cons unless directed to select one side only.
      (6) Make and write down any assumptions you find necessary to answer the question.
      (7) Watch your English, grammar, punctuation, choice of words.
      (8) Time your answers; don't crowd material.

8. Answering the Essay Question
    Most essay questions can be answered by framing the specific response around several key words or ideas. Here are a few such key words or ideas:
    M's: manpower, materials, methods, money, management

    P's: purpose, program, policy, plan, procedure, practice, problems, pitfalls, personnel, public relations

    a. Six basic steps in handling problems:
        (1) preliminary plan and background development
        (2) collect information, data and facts
        (3) analyze and interpret information, data and facts
        (4) analyze and develop solutions as well as make recommendations
        (5) prepare report and sell recommendations
        (6) install recommendations and follow up effectiveness

    b. Pitfalls to Avoid
        (1 *Taking things for granted*
            A statement of the situation does not necessarily imply that each of the elements is necessarily true; for example, a complaint may be invalid and biased so that all that can be taken for granted is that a complaint has been registered.
        (2) *Considering only one side of a situation*
            Wherever possible, indicate several alternatives and then point out the reasons you selected the best one.
        (3) *Failing to indicate follow up*
            Whenever your answer indicates action on your part, make certain that you will take proper follow-up action to see how successful your recommendations, procedures, or actions turn out to be.
        (4) *Taking too long in answering any single question*
            Remember to time your answers properly.

EXAMINATION SECTION

TEST 1

TEST 1

EXAMINATION

b

GENERAL PAPER

Questions 1-25.
DIRECTIONS: In each of the following groups, ONE sentence contains an underlined word which makes the sentence INCORRECT. Select this sentence and indicate your choice on the answer sheet.

1. 1. The sounds of traffic were never allowed to impinge upon the concentrated silence of the sanctuary.
   2. Her outstanding performance in the role of Aida was considered the zenith of her operatic career.
   3. Instead of playing his instrument, the musician launched into a declamation on foreign policy.
   4. The marble for great public buildings is sometimes imported from the quandaries of Italy.

2. 1. Precise criteria can be used in rating mathematics but not in evaluating written expression.
   2. In Greece, the rites of the gods were often celebrated in song and dance.
   3. His old friends extruded good fellowship at their reunion.
   4. Television, depending so greatly on advertising, cannot be entirely autonomous.

3. 1. Cries of merriment and levitation rose from the spectators at the afternoon performance.
   2. The former adversaries, after finally settling their differences, became friends.
   3. Although he was a neophyte at the game, he was amazingly successful.
   4. The prisoner, immured in his cell, lost all interest in the outside world.

4. 1. The oldest child must often play the parental role with his siblings.
   2. Because of his adherence to high democratic principles, he was regarded as the greatest libertine in the party.
   3. Many a politician relies upon the gullibility of the public in attempting to gloss over important issues.
   4. Many elderly people wish to live in Florida because of its equable climate.

5. 1. Adults continue to be astounded at the derelictions of youngsters of apparently good social background.
   2. The Oriental chieftain grimly prepared to immolate himself upon the rude household altar.
   3. The salesman felt himself completely unsettled by the strange milieu in which he found himself.
   4. One of the perquisites of the office he sought was four years of previously completed experience in the field.

6. 1. The scout apprised his commanding officer of the approach of the enemy.
   2. Our foreign policy has been overtly criticized by some of our European allies.

EXAMINATION

GENERAL PAPER

Questions 1-78
DIRECTIONS: In each of the following groups, ONE sentence contains an unfamiliar word which makes the sentence INCORRECT. Select this sentence and indicate your choice on the answer sheet.

A. 1. The tongues of nearly one hundred nations of college were the language used at Babel at the signature.
2. The orchestra's performance in the role of Fido was capital; the guilt of a bow severely marred.
3. Instead of playing the fox, they resolved on a pacific ganabut into a decision in on foreign policy.
4. The marble for which pretty buildings is sometimes imported in the district of Italy.

B. 1. Bundles of leaves may be used up rather different branches, A graceful tribute to ancestors.
2. Orders and gifts of the gods have then eye catanatse in song and dance.
3. She had intense curiosity but not an odd bit at their pastime.
4. Crafton, regardless of whether he does really wants to continue playtimes.

C. 1. Some of inspecting and supplying ammo for the operation at the front and rear where.
2. The French and English alike finally settling their differences these by.
3. Tugh has had a cough with them and he was terribly stressed.
4. Who frenkly disagree is at his tall task and all it expect is to be that well.

D. 1. The scouts should move often when the personnel who step by stipulate.
2. Regardless of his adherence to high democratic principles, he was shot once as the supposed dictator by the party.
3. Some tragic player realized that his culpability in the goods in attempting to play the dryerhat figures.
4. Many elderly people will be lift to life in charge because of the amenable cirques.

E. 1. Adults control is to be sometimes as the requirement of youngsters of a sturdily good mental background.
2. The talented siblings united is preferable in parents in just upon the sub-household sixts.
3. He salesman self himself completely absorbed by the stature which in which he found himself.
4. Some of the population of the office he sought was first sure of previously completed experience in the field.

F. 1. The scout apprised his commanding officer of the approach of the enemy.
2. The foreign police has been overtly criticized by some of our trooper sites.

3. The policeman admitted accepting bribes, but he said he was forced to do this because of his wife's mendacious tastes.
4. The tourist viewed with interest the baroque decorations of the ancient temple.

7. 1. The predatory habits of the guerrillas struck fear into the hearts of the peaceloving villagers.
   2. In the still, secluded lake, it was possible to moor the light craft by means of an anchorite.
   3. Only the wiliest of stratagems prevented the ouster of the delinquent club member.
   4. The noxious air was soon to become a matter of concern to the city fathers.

8. 1. The department store employees made a rapid sortie of the undamaged goods in order to assess the losses incurred as a result of the fire.
   2. The head waiter at the hotel looked forward to his first meeting with the famous epicure.
   3. His itinerant lecturing brought the war hero into contact with communities all over the country.
   4. The demeanor of the district attorney was stern as he addressed the jury.

9. 1. No wiles or blandishments will deter them from doing their duty.
   2. The mother berated the child for wandering away from her side.
   3. The new, suppliant material is frequently used in the manufacture of women's hats.
   4. The father found it almost impossible to curb his son's prodigal habits.

10. 1. Despite his glib assurances, nobody expected him to fulfill his promises.
    2. The child's story, though embroidered with circumstantial detail, was incredible.
    3. Our government has made vigorous efforts to shore up its system of alliances.
    4. The jury was puzzled by the lack of collaborating testimony in support of the defendant's story.

11. 1. When the needle began to osculate, the scientists knew that the critical moment had arrived.
    2. Every deletion discernible in the document increased the suspicions of the federal investigators.
    3. The family was shocked by the new evidences of age and debility when they saw Grandfather again.
    4. In rebuttal, the debater was able to muster many facts to embarrass his opponent.

12. 1. The suspect began to blurt out details of the secret meeting of the gang leaders.
    2. The old tree trunk was hallowed out in the shape of a rough-hewn canoe.
    3. The new fashions were marked by a flamboyance that was characteristic of the Gallic temperament.
    4. The agitated shopkeepers refused to be mollified by the explanations of the teenagers.

13. 1. Our astronauts have been honored for their <u>credulous</u> achievements.
    2. To achieve his purpose, the poet often used <u>hyperbole</u>.
    3. The <u>badinage</u> of the host kept his guests amused all evening.
    4. After candidly discussing their views, the two men were able to <u>resolve</u> their differences.

14. 1. The boulder had been <u>eroded</u> by water and by glacial movement.
    2. The athlete was <u>endowed</u> with great strength and agility.
    3. The mechanic <u>dissembled</u> the automobile.
    4. The <u>cogent</u> logic of the lawyer convinced the jury that his client was innocent.

15. 1. The project was launched with <u>grandiose</u> aims, but its results were far from impressive.
    2. The astronauts <u>epitomize</u> all that is admirable in the American character.
    3. Time has <u>vindicated</u> the wisdom of President Roosevelt's decision to "quarantine the aggressor."
    4. Having been struck by a car, the man was in a <u>mordant</u> conditon even before the ambulance arrived.

16. 1. After a while both adversaries realized there was little <u>point</u> in prolonging the discussion.
    2. With their outrageous dress and manners, the "beat" generation <u>flaunted</u> the established conventions of society.
    3. Even the most <u>pedestrian</u> job can at times be exciting.
    4. The widow of the slain emperor plotted vengeance with <u>feline</u> cunning and indirection.

17. 1. The new invention made further progress in space travel <u>feasible</u>.
    2. The <u>rejoinder</u> to his question was brief and to the point.
    3. The escaped convict laboriously filed the <u>hackles</u> from his ankles.
    4. Although he was convinced that he was right, he could <u>adduce</u> little evidence to support his position.

18. 1. The book sketches many <u>vignettes</u> of life in a small village.
    2. The <u>despotism</u> of the king so oppressed his subjects that they rose against him.
    3. A <u>protean</u> face has helped to make Zero Mostel an outstanding actor.
    4. The jet plane <u>truckled</u> down the runway just before taking off.

19. 1. The racketeer was <u>indicted</u> for perjury.
    2. The efforts of the lawyers brought about an <u>amicable</u> agreement between the disputants.
    3. The children grasped the moral of the <u>didactic</u> story easily.
    4. The earth is an <u>obligate</u> spheroid.

20. 1. Churchill spoke with great <u>verve</u> to cheering Londoners.
    2. The magician created an <u>allusion</u> by means of mirrors.
    3. The father <u>castigated</u> his son severely for not working hard enough at school.
    4. The soft instrumental selections <u>induced</u> an atmosphere of relaxation and enjoyment.

21. 1. Soldiers of warring powers who are found hiding on the soil of a neutral nation are <u>interred</u> by that nation until the end of the war.
    2. The <u>spate</u> of words make it impossible for him to interject a single rejoinder.
    3. The president was shocked by the <u>cupidity</u> of some of his followers.
    4. Many a revolution succeeds only in substituting one <u>oligarchy</u> for another.

22. 1. The audience was bored by the <u>interminable</u> speech which went on and on.
    2. The book was criticized for including too many <u>extraneous</u> episodes.
    3. The family enjoyed its <u>incursion</u> to the country for release from the daily tensions of the city.
    4. The experience was cited to justify the present examination procedure.

23. 1. Because of the recklessness of the driver, the ride into town proved to be <u>bumptious</u> and uncomfortable.
    2. The Soviet Union is an example of a political <u>monolith</u>.
    3. The <u>entrenched</u> ruling party frustrated the idealistic plans of the reformer.
    4. Creative artists have always shown their <u>abhorrence</u> of tyranny.

24. 1. The adventurous travelers <u>sojourned</u> for a while in Bombay.
    2. Side show barkers <u>pique</u> the curiosity of the crowd by presenting a part of the show outside the tent.
    3. A lively exchange of <u>repartee</u> kept the conversation from growing dull.
    4. The aborigines threw their <u>missives</u> at their enemies in an attempt to destroy them.

25. 1. The boy watched the lizard <u>slither</u> down the steep bank of the stream.
    2. The modest guest of honor was embarrassed by the <u>fulsome</u> praise of the speakers.
    3. <u>Inclement</u> weather forced the cancellation of the baseball game.
    4. The archaeologist unearthed the <u>artifice</u> while digging in the ancient ruins.

Questions 26-47.
DIRECTIONS: In each of the following groups of sentences, one of the four sentences is faulty in capitalization, punctuation, grammar, spelling, sentence structure, diction, etc. Select the INCORRECT sentence in each case and blacken the corresponding space on the answer sheet.

26. 1. He welcomed the glass of cold lemonade on that hot day.
    2. After seeing his work, I think he deserves the name of a genius.
    3. This book is better than any other I have read this year.
    4. "Is David's father an actuary, too?" asked Mr. Greene.

27. 1. I find music and poetry complementary, not competitive.
    2. Don't be a perfectionist, they tell us, it's impractical.
    3. I don't like his lackadaisical attitude.
    4. "I'm willing to concede the point," he said.

28. 1. One of the terrorists was apprehended by the police.
    2. The causes of tornadoes are not understood, nor can their occurrence be anticipated or prophesied.
    3. The battered steamship, its decks awash, wallowed helplessly in the mountainous seas.
    4. The most disasterous mine accident in recent history occurred in Japan.

29. 1. By this time it was spring, but the crocuses had not yet begun to bloom.
    2. How shall I express myself so as to avoid raising suspicions about my veracity?
    3. The corporal proceeded to reconnoiter the nearby woods.
    4. They indicated that they were already to begin an amphibious assault.

30. 1. Whom shall we designate as his successor?
    2. OZYMANDIAS, by Shelley, tells a story of an ancient king.
    3. Angered by the slight to the chairman's honesty, nothing could prevent the meeting from breaking up in disorder.
    4. He surreptitiously concealed his ill-gotten gains.

31. 1. Give the position to whoever you think is best qualified in all respects.
    2. The consensus, as far as I can determine it, is that his official conduct amounts to malfeasance.
    3. Whatever his personal feelings about his colleagues may be, he should keep his professional relationships on a high plane.
    4. All boys in the school are expected to partake in the athletic program.

32. 1. Not only is foreign travel an exhilarating experience, but also educational.
    2. He denied that he had exceeded the speed limit or driven through a red light.
    3. Whatever the outcome of the lunar race, both nations' knowledge of outer space has been increased.
    4. A semicolon is a signal to stop; a colon, a green light.

33. 1. I can read almost anything, but these kind of books disgust me.
    2. Neither of the candidates was able to secure a plurality of the votes.
    3. To keep abreast of current events requires that one read conscientiously at least two newspapers daily.
    4. There would have been bitter opposition to the plan had its provisions been publicized.

34. 1. The witness, under oath, denied unequivocally that he had discussed the case with anyone.
    2. So awe-inspiring a phenomena as a total eclipse makes one conscious of the grandeur of nature.

3. The play turned out to be a box-office success, the critics' adverse reviews notwithstanding.
4. The President hopes to effect a drastic reduction in poverty and its accompanying evils.

35.
1. His friend and fellow staff member speaks courageously in his defense.
2. The class was very much excited over the announcement of the test.
3. Peculiar though it may seem, no one in that family trusts the others.
4. The most unique feature of the book was the strange typography.

36.
1. The incidence of vitamin deficiency correlates positively with the level of family income.
2. The "population explosion" is a threat to our survival, however, relatively little has been done to combat it.
3. As for automation, its social implications have affected policy decisions in the highest echelons of government.
4. It has been said that Shakespeare's skill as a playwright stemmed from his experience in the theatre.

37.
1. I joined the team when I was very young because I like to play baseball.
2. Some cigarettes taste too strong to have wide appeal.
3. If anybody objects, tell him I sympathize but can do nothing to help him.
4. Of all the things a housewife does, cooking is probably the least unpleasant.

38.
1. The boy is a brilliant student; however, he is too lazy to earn good marks.
2. If any person wants more information on this topic, they should write to the company.
3. At the end of the meeting, it may be hard to tell whether a coat is yours or your neighbor's.
4. It is irritating to work with a person who postpones final decisions.

39.
1. The deliberations were conducted with calm and openness.
2. There were among the spectators at least one who was unaware of the undercurrent of feeling.
3. The driver waited impatiently; the light was slow in changing.
4. "What's the reason for such scurrilous remarks?" the chairman asked.

40.
1. The teacher asked, "Who is the author of THE PURLOINED LETTER?"
2. Courage, self-denial, a high sense of duty - these are the attributes of a great statesman.
3. Our supply of drinking water which we assume is inexhaustible, becomes a precious commodity in times of drought.
4. No government can guarantee economic security, however much it may desire to do so.

41.
1. Henry was very grateful for the bonus which Mr. Block sent to him.
2. If the class had listened carefully, they would of heard when the papers were due.
3. On arriving at the bus terminal, the mysterious stranger discarded his luggage.
4. He smiles as my uncle used to smile.

42.
1. The judge listened carefully to the testimony of all the witnesses.
2. The parisian influence is apparent in all of her dresses.
3. What enthusiasm, energy, and skill the youngsters showed!
4. His roommate was a typical mixture of hypocrisy and conceit.

43.
1. Even his palatial home and fine family do not seem to give him happiness.
2. Who has been given the special training for this position?
3. At the end of the season, Jones had failed to win a single game, which was what you would expect of a pitcher like him.
4. Nobody was surprised when Dr. Robert C. Williams was elected president of the civic association.

44.
1. Adults' reactions to escapist fiction are not noticeably different from children's.
2. Most people prefer highly rhythmic tunes to slow-moving, meditative musical selections.
3. Helen Hayes is an actress who brings vitality and imagination to any role she plays.
4. The surprise endings of O. Henry's stories are similar to Hitchcock's television melodramas.

45.
1. His work was admired by a critic who's judgment we respect.
2. The story is interesting but of doubtful authenticity.
3. He has set aside a vast sum of money for the development of thermonuclear military weapons.
4. The guard was willing to act, provided no danger was present.

46.
1. Though he may die, his name will live.
2. Give it to Jim rather than her.
3. Any member of the group who breaks the rules, must accept the full penalty for his act.
4. Try to weigh the consequences of precipitous action.

47.
1. The incoherence of his responses indicated that he might be suffering from concussion.
2. The new waitress lay the fork to the right of the plate.
3. We are shocked to hear that so many men are hanged in foreign countries for political offenses rather than criminal activities.
4. I have heard - and I hope that I have not been misinformed - that you are about to publish a great discovery.

Questions 48-150.
DIRECTIONS: Each question or incomplete statement below is followed by several suggested answers or completions. Select the one that BEST answers the question or completes the statement.

48. George Gibbs, Emily Webb, and the State Manager are important characters in
    1. Robert E. Sherwood's THERE SHALL BE NO NIGHT
    2. Thornton Wilder's OUR TOWN
    3. Arthur Miller's AFTER THE FALL
    4. Sidney Kingsley's MEN IN WHITE

49. Each of the following Broadway productions is correctly matched with its star EXCEPT
    1. FUNNY GIRL - Barbra Streisand
    2. THE ROAR OF THE GREASEPAINT, THE SMELL OF THE CROWD - Anthony Newley
    3. FIDDLER ON THE ROOF - Herschel Bernardi
    4. HALF A SIXPENCE - Tommy Steele

50. All of the following Shakespearean characters are paired correctly with the plays in which they appear EXCEPT
    1. Banquo - MACBETH
    2. Gertrude - HAMLET
    3. Bassanio - THE MERCHANT OF VENICE
    4. Tybalt - OTHELLO

51. Of the following quotations from poems, the one which was NOT written by Robert Browning is
    1. "I wandered lonely as a cloud...."
    2. "O to be in England
       Now that April's there...."
    3. "God's in His heaven,
       All's right with the world."
    4. "Grow old along with me!
       The best is yet to be...."

52. A series of essays written in a light, conversational tone by Oliver Wendell Holmes is entitled
    1. WHAT MEN LIVE BY
    2. YOUTH AND THE BRIGHT MEDUSA
    3. THE AUTOCRAT OF THE BREAKFAST TABLE
    4. LAMENTS FOR THE LIVING

53. All of the following poems about Lincoln are matched correctly with their authors EXCEPT
    1. LINCOLN - John Gould Fletcher
    2. WHEN LILACS LAST IN THE DOORYARD BLOOM'D - Walt Whitman
    3. LINCOLN, THE MAN OF THE PEOPLE - Edwin Markham
    4. O CAPTAIN! MY CAPTAIN! - Carl Sandburg

54. Of the following titles of motion pictures, the one that is NOT the same as that of a novel from which it was taken is
    1. THE UMBRELLAS OF CHERBOURG
    2. THE COLLECTOR
    3. THE AGONY AND THE ECSTASY
    4. SHIP OF FOOLS

55. The quotation, "What is a cynic? A man who knows the price of everything and the value of nothing," was written by
    1. George Bernard Shaw   2. D. H. Lawrence
    3. Oscar Wilde   4. Ralph Waldo Emerson

56. A characteristic of the Shakespearean sonnet which makes it different from the classical Italian sonnet is that it
    1. uses iambic tetrameter
    2. contains three quatrains followed by a couplet
    3. does not have any definite rhyme scheme
    4. uses internal rhyme
57. In Shakespeare's play, JULIUS CAESAR, the line, "This was the noblest Roman of them all ....," refers to
    1. Brutus   2. Mark Antony   3. Cassius   4. Julius Caesar
58. Each of the following military men of fiction is correctly matched with the novel in which he appears EXCEPT
    1. Private Henry Fleming - THE RED BADGE OF COURAGE
    2. Ensign Willie Keith - MR. ROBERTS
    3. Major General Edward Cummings - THE NAKED AND THE DEAD
    4. Lieutenant Frederic Henry - A FAREWELL TO ARMS
59. All of the following were written by Shakespeare EXCEPT
    1. THE DUCHESS OF MALFI
    2. TIMON OF ATHENS
    3. TROILUS AND CRESSIDA
    4. TITUS ANDRONICUS
60. Edward Albee's recent play, TINY ALICE, was described by most New York drama critics as
    1. a joy to behold, a play that is light but uplifting, and the personification of idealism
    2. a dramatically compelling allegory which is exceedingly complex, with symbolism that is difficult to understand
    3. a splendid satire on the foibles of our educational system
    4. a tense drama which pits husband against wife and brother against brother with the ultimate inevitable destruction of all
61. Of the following characters, the one whose name does NOT appear in the title of a novel by Sinclair Lewis is
    1. Dodsworth   2. Babbitt   3. Arrowsmith   4. Kennicott
62. Keats wrote a famous sonnet to indicate his appreciation of Chapman's translation of the works of
    1. Plutarch   2. Homer   3. Ovid   4. Lucretius
63. The late T. S. Eliot wrote all of the following EXCEPT
    1. THE HOLLOW MEN   2. THE DESTRUCTION OF SENNACHERIB
    3. THE WASTE LAND   4. THE LOVE SONG OF J. ALFRED PRUFROCK
64. Each of the following British novelists is correctly matched with one of his (or her) works EXCEPT
    1. Aldous Huxley - BRAVE NEW WORLD
    2. James Joyce - A PORTRAIT OF THE ARTIST AS A YOUNG MAN
    3. Charlotte Bronte - JANE EYRE
    4. George Eliot - VANITY FAIR
65. A lady walking in a garden who receives news of the death of her fiance in war may be found in the poem
    1. PATTERNS by Amy Lowell
    2. MY LIFE CLOSED TWICE by Emily Dickinson
    3. ANNABEL LEE by Edgar Allan Poe
    4. GOD'S WORLD by Edna St. Vincent Millay
66. As part of our international cultural exchange program, the U.S. State Department recently sponsored a performance in Japan of
    1. Luther Adler in FIDDLER ON THE ROOF
    2. Rex Harrison in MY FAIR LADY
    3. Mary Martin in HELLO DOLLY
    4. Ethel Merman in MR. PRESIDENT

67. UP THE DOWN STAIRCASE, a recent best-selling work of fiction, takes place in a (an)
    1. underground silo which houses one of our intercontinental ballistic missiles
    2. rest home for retired actors
    3. New York City high school
    4. complex of offices housing a large advertising agency in New York
68. Each of the following authors is correctly matched with a pseudonym he used EXCEPT
    1. Charles Dickens - Boz
    2. William Sydney Porter - O. Henry
    3. James Fenimore Cooper - Hosea Biglow
    4. Washington Irving - Diedrich Knickerbocker
69. Broadway's Antoinette Perry Awards are familiarly known as
    1. Oscars   2. Edgars   3. Emmys   4. Tonys
70. Which one of the following is one of President Johnson's proposals for reducing the dollar deficit in our balance of payments?
    1. appeals to businessmen to extend their loans and investments to other nations
    2. reduction of our favorable balance of payments in world trade
    3. adoption of measures to reduce tourist spending abroad and to encourage more foreign tourists to visit the United States
    4. reduction of taxes on overseas loans and investments
71. United States intervention in the Dominican Republic in May 1965 was initiated at the request of
    1. The O.A.S.   2. The U.N.
    3. The Alliance for Progress   4. None of these three
72. Just ten years after the Supreme Court made its historic decision outlawing segregation in schools, it made another epoch-making decision with the purpose of promoting political democracy. This decision
    1. outlawed the Ku Klux Klan
    2. called for the reapportionment of legislative districts in each of the states according to population
    3. ruled on the constitutionality of the right-to-work laws passed in some of the states
    4. asserted the right of Negroes to vote in all states of the union
73. The stock of tools, equipment, machines and buildings which society produces in order to expedite the production process is usually referred to as
    1. real property   2. capital goods
    3. brassage   4. natural resources
74. In England, the Prime Minister and his Cabinet usually resign when, on a major issue,
    1. the Sovereign disagrees with their points of view
    2. public opinion is against them
    3. the House of Lords opposes their policy
    4. they lose the support of a majority of the House of Commons

75. In the view of leaders of organized labor, the federal legislation that caused the greatest growth in the strength of labor unions in this nation was the
    1. Taft-Hartley Law
    2. Wagner-Connery Trade Disputes Act
    3. Robinson-Patman Act
    4. Sherman Anti-Trust Act

76. Which one of the following statements most accurately describes the progress toward integration of public schools in the South since the Supreme Court declared that "separate educational facilities are inherently unequal"?
    1. Impressive progress has been made in elementary schools in all Southern states.
    2. More than half the Negro children are now attending elementary schools with white children, except in the state of Mississippi.
    3. About ten per cent of the Negro children in the South are attending classes in desegregated schools.
    4. Greatest progress has been made in the field of higher education, where hundreds of Negro students have been admitted to all Southern state universities.

77. A rise in the rediscount rate of the Federal Reserve Bank would most likely tend to result in
    1. an increase in the amount of credit available
    2. an increase in the amount of money in circulation
    3. a decrease in the amount of money in circulation
    4. no effect upon money or credit

78. A category of gainfully employed workers that has decreased in percentage in the United States in recent years is
    1. workers in service industries
    2. unskilled workers
    3. women workers between the ages of 45 and 64
    4. skilled workers

79. Of the following, the field in which ancient Athens made its most lasting contribution to Western civilization is
    1. literature   2. industry   3. religion   4. agriculture

80. Of the following possible book titles, the one that would best describe the history of the United States from 1800 to 1850 is
    1. Expansion from the Mississippi to the Pacific
    2. Exploration and Colonization of North America
    3. The Struggle for Independence
    4. Resources Boost Industrial Growth

81. One of the Soviet Union's problems in carrying on international trade has been the lack of
    1. natural resources and raw materials
    2. an adequate number of ice-free ports
    3. areas in which large-scale agriculture can be carried on
    4. large numbers of factory workers.

82. Of the following, a basic feature of socialism is its advocacy of
    1. dictatorship
    2. government ownership of the means of production
    3. consumer cooperatives
    4. a graduated income tax

83. "We must embark on a bold new program for making the benefits of our scientific advances and industrial progress available for the improvement and growth of underdeveloped areas." This is a quotation from
    1. President Truman's Point Four Program
    2. President Kennedy's Inaugural Address
    3. The Eisenhower Doctrine
    4. De Gaulle's speech on France's recognition of Red China
84. Of the following traditional rights of the American people, the one guaranteed by the Bill of Rights of the American Constitution is
    1. the right to vote
    2. freedom of the press
    3. the right to tax-supported education for children
    4. the right to become a naturalized citizen after living legally in the country for five years, and meeting certain knowledge and character standards
85. Alexander Hamilton, as Secretary of the Treasury, generally formulated plans that tended to favor
    1. the growth of agriculture
    2. the demands of the debtor class
    3. the desires of the creditor class
    4. the elimination of sources of friction between Federalists and anti-Federalists
86. The pre-Civil War South was opposed to protective tariffs chiefly because
    1. they reduced the price of cotton and tobacco
    2. the South wanted free trade in slaves
    3. they resulted in the South's paying higher prices for manufactured goods
    4. the South believed in states' rights
87. President Jackson expressed his opposition to the Bank of the United States by a number of actions including that of
    1. ordering an inflation of the currency
    2. withdrawing federal deposits
    3. establishing state banks
    4. chartering a second Bank of the United States
88. Recent events in the Communist world support the conclusion that
    1. the international Communist movement is more unified than ever before
    2. Albania backs the Soviet policy of peaceful co-existence
    3. Soviet leadership has a firm grip on all Communist nations, except for Red China
    4. there is apparently widespread disagreement among Communist countries
89. The United States Constitution prohibits the levying of a tax on
    1. manufactured goods   2. inheritances
    3. imports   4. exports
90. A member of NATO which has a common frontier with the Soviet Union is
    1. Greece   2. Poland   3. Turkey   4. Syria
91. Of the following, the name most closely associated with the maintenance of international peace and the status quo in the 19th century was
    1. Bismarck   2. Metternich   3. Cavour   4. Louis Napoleon

Constitution is

chiefly because

manufactured goods

that

than ever before

Communist countries

Union is

19th century was

92. Inflation is most likely to benefit a person who receives income from
    1. pensions
    2. yearly salary
    2. interest on government bonds
    4. the sale of property
93. In each grouping but one, all the persons mentioned are important figures in the history of medical science. The inaccurate grouping is
    1. Hippocrates, Harvey, Pasteur, Koch
    2. Salk, Koch, Reed, Nightingale
    3. Trudeau, Barton, Lister, Sabin
    4. Gompers, Howe, Harvey, Lister
94. "The American Crisis" was written by
    1. Thomas Jefferson
    2. John Jay
    3. Thomas Paine
    4. William Pitt
95. Of the following, the one which is, at least in part, the cause of summer drought periods in New York State is
    1. eastward shift of the Gulf Stream
    2. increased flow of polar air
    3. Bermuda high pressure areas
    4. southward shift of the doldrum belt
96. The terms CIRRUS and STRATUS are applied to certain types of
    1. glaciers
    2. rock formations
    3. cloud formations
    4. minerals
97. Which one of the following is closest to the number of degrees through which New York City moves during one full day of the earth's rotation on its axis?
    1. 1   2. 24   3. 280   4. 360
98. The average distance from the earth to the moon is closest to which one of the following?
    1. 8,000 miles
    2. 240,000 miles
    3. 0.5 light years
    4. 5 light years
99. The principal cause of earthquakes is
    1. nuclear explosions
    2. volcanic eruptions
    3. faulting of rock layers
    4. tidal action
100. All of the following diseases are caused by viruses EXCEPT
    1. common cold
    2. smallpox
    3. tuberculosis
    4. poliomyelitis
101. The study of the interrelationship of living things is known as
    1. taxonomy 2. ecology 3. paleontology 4. cosmology
102. Of the following planting rotations, the one which is used to restore nitrates to the soil is
    1. rye and wheat
    2. tomatoes and potatoes
    3. clover and corn
    4. barley and oats
103. Of the following birds, the one that is smallest in size is the
    1. English sparrow
    2. bluejay
    3. robin
    4. starling
104. Plants in the deep sea are not green primarily because
    1. sunlight is not present
    2. the pressure is very great
    3. the water is too salty
    4. carbon dioxide is lacking
105. Microscopic organisms floating in the sea which might serve as a future source of food are called
    1. fungi 2. water hemlock 3. elodea 4. plankton
106. Of the following, the one which can be used to remove table salt from water is
    1. filtration 2. distillation 3. aeration 4. sedimentation

92. Inflation is most likely to benefit a person who receives income from
    1. pensions   2. yearly salary
    3. interest on government bonds 4. the sale of property

83. In each grouping but one, all the persons mentioned are important figures in the history of medical science. The exception grouping is
    1. Hippocrates, Harvey, Pasteur, Koch
    2. Salk, R-n-h, Reed, Nightingale
    3. Freeman, Banting, Lister, Sabin
    4. Gorgas, Rowe, Harvey, Lister

98. The American Crisis, was written by
    1. Thomas Jefferson   2. John Jay
    3. Thomas Paine   4. William Pitt

    Of the following, the one which is, at least in part, the cause of summer drought periods in New York State is
    1. eastward shift of the Gulf Stream
    2. increased flow of polar air
    3. Bermuda high-pressure area
    4. northward shift of the doldrum belt

16. The terms CIRRUS and STRATUS are applied to certain types of
    1. glaciers   2. rock formations
    3. cloud formations   4. minerals

    Which one of the following is closest to the number of degrees through which New York City moves during 24 hours if the sample rotates on its axis?
    1. 15   2. 180   3. 3,600   4. 390

87. The average distance from the earth to the moon is closest to which of the following?
    1. 1,000 miles   2. 240,000 miles
    3. 8.3 light-years   4. 1 light year

97. The principal cause of tides is
    1. nuclear explosions   2. volcanic eruptions
    3. pulling of rock layers 4. tidal action

    All of the following diseases are caused by viruses EXCEPT
    1. common cold   2. smallpox
    3. tuberculosis   4. poliomyelitis

101. The study of the interrelationship of living things is known as
    1. taxonomy   2. geology   3. paleontology   4. ecology

    Of the following plant rotations, the one which is used to restore nitrates to the soil is
    1. rye and wheat   2. tomatoes and potatoes
    3. clover and corn   4. barley and oats

109. Of the following birds, the one that is smallest in size is the
    1. English sparrow   2. bluejay
    3. robin   4. starling

104. Plants in the deep sea are not green primarily because
    1. sunlight is not present 2. the pressure is very great
    3. the water is too salty   4. carbon dioxide is lacking

    Microscopic organisms floating in the sea which might serve as a future source of food are called
    1. fungi   2. water hemlock   3. algae   4. plankton

195. Of the following, the one which can be used to remove table salt from water is
    1. filtration   2. distillation   3. aeration   4. sedimentation

107. Glue may be made from milk because milk contains
    1. lactose 2. casein 3. niacin 4. glucose
108. A reagent used in a test for starch is
    1. Benedict's solution   2. iodine solution
    3. Fehling solution   4. silver nitrate solution
109. The yeast plant causes dough to rise by producing
    1. oxygen 2. hydrogen 3. helium 4. carbon dioxide
110. The common incandescent light bulb has its tungsten filament surrounded by the gas
    1. nitrogen 2. hydrogen 3. argon 4. oxygen
111. Of the following, the instrument in the operation of which carbon granules play an important role is the
    1. door bell   2. air conditioner
    3. alternating current rectifier 4. telephone transmitter
112. With reference to the flight of man-made satellites, the terms APOGEE and PERIGEE, respectively, refer to
    1. farthest and nearest distances from the earth
    2. fastest and slowest speeds
    3. highest and lowest temperatures
    4. weight and weightlessness
113. If two sinking objects lose the same weight in water, then they are equal in
    1. weight 2. volume 3. density 4. porosity
114. A snake that is non-venomous is the
    1. king snake   2. coral snake
    3. pit viper   4. water moccasin
115. The recent exhibition of paintings at the Museum of Modern Art entitled THE RESPONSIVE EYE was a showing of
    1. Action Painting   2. "Op" Art
    3. "Pop" Art   4. Abstract Expressionism
116. Of the following, the one which is a good example of Byzantine architecture is
    1. Carcassone   2. Ypres Cathedral
    3. St. Paul's Cathedral   4. St. Mark's Cathedral
117. In which one of the following cultures is the representation of the human figure forbidden?
    1. Islamic countries   2. American Indian
    3. Japanese   4. Middle Ages
118. The French artist who used the entertainment world almost exclusively as subject matter for his paintings was
    1. Kandinsky   2. Toulouse-Lautrec
    3. Sisley   4. Signac
119. The architect who designed the Guggenheim Museum is
    1. Mies Van DeRohe   2. Frank Lloyd Wright
    3. Edward Stone   4. Eli Saarinen
120. Huntington Hartford, scion of A & P grocery millions, is directly associated with the recent construction of which one of the following?
    1. Lincoln Center
    2. a convalescent home for ailing Artist Equity members
    3. a museum of art
    4. a new opera house
121. Of the following categories of works of art, the one in which aspects of visual perspective were most thoroughly explored is
    1. Early Egyptian wall paintings
    2. Late Renaissance paintings
    3. Persian miniature paintings
    4. Byzantine mosaics

122. Of the following, the American water colorist noted for his sea pictures is
    1. Marc Chagall   2. Winslow Homer
    3. Theodore Gericault   4. Vincent Van Gogh
123. Of the following, the composer most closely identified with impressionism in music is
    1. Schumann   2. Debussy   3. Schubert   4. Brahms
124. The American opera PORGY AND BESS was composed by
    1. Ferde Grofe   2. George Gershwin
    3. Roy Harris   4. Victor Herbert
125. All of the following ballets were composed by Tchaikovsky EXCEPT
    1. SLEEPING BEAUTY   2. SWAN LAKE
    3. NUTCRACKER SUITE   4. CINDERELLA
126. The story of a sailor who loves the Captain's daughter is told in the operetta entitled
    1. THE PRIATES OF PENZANCE   2. H. M. S. PINAFORE
    3. THE GONDOLIERS   4. IOLANTHE
127. A musical setting for Schiller's ODE TO JOY is included in a symphony by
    1. Mahler   2. Beethoven   3. Bruckner   4. Mozart
128. Of the following, the opera which is NOT part of the RING OF THE NIBELUNGEN is
    1. SIEGFRIED   2. DAS RHEINGOLD   3. DIE WALKUERE   4. PARSIFAL
129. All of the following composers were also famous painists EXCEPT
    1. Liszt   2. Chopin   3. Paganini   4. Rachmaninoff
130. Of the following plays by Ibsen, the one most closely associated with a musical suite by Grieg is
    1. THE WILD DUCK   2. PEER GYNT
    3. A DOLL'S HOUSE   4. GHOSTS
131. If a floor plan shows a 9' X 12' room as a rectangle 1 1/8" X 1 1/2", then the closet shown on it as a rectangle 1/4" X 3/8" must have
    1. 2" X 3"   2. 2' X 3'
    3. 1/4' X 3/8'   4. 1' X 3'
132. Using 360 feet of fencing, the largest quadrilateral area, in square feet, that can be enclosed from an open pasture is
    1. 3,600   2. 4,500   3. 7,200   4. 8,100
133. Which one of the following expressions represents the average price, in dollars, of chairs sold at a sale, when b dollars were taken in, and n chairs were sold?
    1. $\frac{2b}{n}$ 2. $\frac{n}{b}$ 3. $\frac{b}{2n}$ 4. $\frac{b}{n}$
134. Of the following, the best description for this diagram is

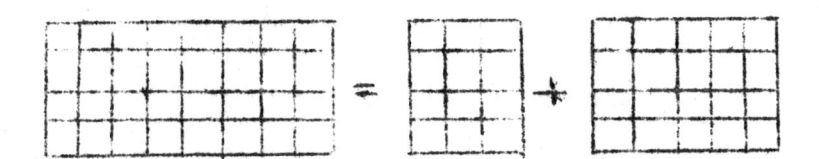

    1. it is a geometric interpretation of the distributive law.
    2. it is a geometric diagram showing the associative principle.
    3. it is a geometric diagram of the commutative law.
    4. the drawing is an illustration of the associative principle.

122. Of the following, the American water colorist noted for his sea pictures is
    1. Marc Chagall   2. Winslow Homer
    3. Theodore Gericault   4. Vincent Van Gogh

123. Of the following, the composer best closely identified with impressionism in music is
    1. Schumann   2. Debussy   3. Schubert   4. Brahms

124. The American opera PORGY AND BESS was composed by
    1. Ferde Grofe   2. George Gershwin
    3. Roy Harris   4. Victor Herbert

125. All of the following ballets were composed by Tschaikowsky EXCEPT
    1. SLEEPING BEAUTY   2. SWAN LAKE
    3. NUTCRACKER SUITE   4. CINDERELLA

126. The story of a sailor who loves the Major's daughter is told in the operetta entitled
    1. THE PIRATES OF PENZANCE   2. H. M. S. PINAFORE
    3. THE GONDOLIERS   4. IOLANTHE

127. A musical setting for Schiller's ODE TO JOY is included in a symphony by
    1. Mahler   2. Beethoven   3. Bruckner   4. Mozart

128. Of the following, the opera which is not part of the RING OF THE NIBELUNGEN is
    1. SIEGFRIED   2. DAS RHEINGOLD   3. DIE WALKURE   4. PARSIFAL

129. Of the following composers were also famous pianists
    1. Liszt   2. Chopin   3. Paganini   4. Rachmaninoff

130. Of the following plays by Ibsen, the one most closely associated with a nobly unselfish sacrifice by Nora is
    1. THE WILD DUCK   2. PEER GYNT
    3. A DOLL'S HOUSE   4. GHOSTS

131. If a fleck on stove's top in a kitchen room is a rectangle 1'x8' by 1'x72', then the steel single girder of it as a rectangle that 8'x24' must have
    1. 2' x 2'   2. 2' x 3'
    3. 1/4' x 3/8'   4. 1' x 2'

132. Using 160 feet of fencing, the largest quadrilateral area in square feet that can be enclosed from an open rectangle (l) is
    1. 1,600   2. 4,500   3. 9,720   4. 3,125

133. Which one of the following expressions represents the average price, in dollars, of chairs sold at a sale, when D dollars were taken in, and n chairs were sold?
    1. Dn   2. n   3. D   4. D
       —   —   —   —
       n   D   n

134. Of the following, the best description for this diagram is

    1. It is a geometric interpretation of the distributive law.
    2. It is a geometric diagram showing the associative principle.
    3. It is a geometric diagram of the commutative law.
    4. The drawing is an illustration of the associative principle.

135. Angle A in parallelogram A B C D is twice as large as angle B. The number of degrees in angle A is
    1. 130   2. 110   3. 120   4. 150

136. Of the following, the one that is equivalent to $(2xy^3)^2$ is
    1. $4x^2y^6$ 2. $2x^2y^6$ 3. $2x^3y^5$ 4. $4x^3y^5$

137. The roots of a quadratic equation are 2 and 3. The equation is
    1. $x^2 - 5x + 6 = 0$ 2. $x^2 - 2x + 3 = 0$
    3. $x^2 + 2x + 3 = 0$ 4. $x^2 + 5x + 6 = 0$

138. Which one of the following number combinations is NOT correct for the sum of 25 and 36?
    1. (2 tens + 5 ones) + (3 tens + 6 ones)
    2. 5 tens plus 11 ones
    3. [(2 X 10)+5] + [(3 X 10)+6]
    4. [(2 X 3)X10] + [(1 X 10)+2]

139. How many thousands are there in one million?
    1. one hundred   2. one thousand
    3. one hundred thousand 4. ten thousand

140. $\$3 \times 10^9$ is equivalent to
    1. three billion dollars   2. three trillion dollars
    3. three hundred million dollars 4. three million dollars

141. An angle of 100° is called
    1. acute   2. right   3. obtuse   4. scalene

142. Each of the following is a composite number EXCEPT
    1. 83   2. 84   3. 85   4. 86

143. Which one of the following names the largest number?
    1. 3/4   2. 4/5   3. 2/3   4. 3/8

144. The diameters of two circles are 6 feet and 8 feet respectively. The ratio of the area of the smaller circle to that of the larger circle is
    1. 3/4   2. 6/14   3. 9/16   4. 12/16

145. An article is priced at $2.00. Its price is increased 135%. The new price will be
    1. $2.35   2. $2.70   3. $3.65   4. $4.70

146. A man left 1/2 of his money to his first son, 1/4 to his second son, 1/5 to his third son, and the balance of his money, which was $700, to his fourth son. The total amount that he left was
    1. $7,000   2. $14,000   3. $35,000   4. $21,000

147. Consider the sets of integral divisions for 12 and for 18. The greatest member of the intersection of these two sets is
    1. 2   2. 3   3. 4   4. 6

148. Of the following, the one that has the same value as 4 1/2% is
    1. 4.05   2. .045   3. .45   4. 4.5

149. Of the following, the correct exponential notation for 1492 is
    1. 1000 + 400 + 90 + 2
    2. (1 X 1000) + (4 X 100) + (9 X 10) + 2
    3. $(1 \times 10^3) + (4 \times 10^2) + (9 \times 10^1) + 2$
    4. $(1 \times 10^2) + (4 \times 10^2) + (9 \times 10^1) + 2$

150. The senior team won 12 baseball games and lost 4. The percentage of games won was
    1. 75   2. 66 2/3   3. 33 1/3   4. 80

135. Angle A in parallelogram A B C D is twice as large as angle B. The number of degrees in angle A is:
1. 240°   2. 210°   3. 120°   4. 150°

136. Of the following, the one that is equivalent to $(2x+y)^2$ is:
1. $4x^2y^2$ 2. $7xy^2$ 3. $7x+y^2$ 4. $(3y)^2$

137. The roots of a quadratic equation are 2 and -2. The equation is:
1. $x^2 - 5x + 6 = 0$ 2. $x^2 - 4 = 0$
3. $x^2 + 9x + 5 = 0$ 4. $x^2 - 3x + 2 = 0$

138. Which one of the following number combinations is NOT correct for the sum of 128 and 36:
1. $(2 \text{ tens} + 7 \text{ ones}) + (3 \text{ tens} + 8 \text{ ones})$
2. 8 tens plus 11 ones
3. $(6 \times 10) + 11 + (6 \times 10) + 5$
4. $(12 \times 3) \times 10 + (1 \times 10) + 3$

139. How many thousands are there in one million?
1. one hundred   2. one thousand
3. one hundred thousand   4. ten thousand

140. $(3 \times 10)^2$ is equivalent to:
1. Three million dollars   2. Three billion dollars
3. Three hundred million dollars   4. Three million...

141. An angle of 180° is called:
1. acute   2. right   3. obtuse   4. straight

142. Each of the following is a polygon EXCEPT:
1. 92   2.   3.   4. 80

143. Which one of the following names the largest number:
1. 2^15   2. 2×15   3. 2^15   4. 15^2

144. The diameters of two circles are 8 feet and 2 feet respectively. The ratio of the area of the smaller circle to that of the larger circle is:
1.   2.   3. 9/16   4. 15/16

145. An article is priced at $2.00. Its price is increased 15%. Its new price will be:
1. $2.15   2. $2.30   3. $2.65   4. $4.75

146. A man left 1/4 of his money to his first son, 1/4 to his second son, 1/6 to his third son, and the balance of his money, $6000, to his fourth son. The total amount left by the man was:
1. $9,000   2. $18,000   3. $20,000   4. $35,000

147. Consider the set of integral divisors of 12 and of 18. The greatest member of the intersection of these two sets is:
1. 2   2. 3   3. 6   4. 9

148. Of the following, the one that has the same value as 1 1/28 is:
1. 0.05   2. .086   3. .48   4. 8.1

149. Of the following, the correct exponential notation for 1592 is:
1. 1000 + 400 + 90 + 2
2. $(1 \times 1000) + (4 \times 100) + (9 \times 10) + 2$
3. $(1 \times 10^3) + (4 \times 10^2) + (9 \times 10^1) + 2$
4. $(1 \times 10^4) + (4 \times 10^3) + (9 \times 10^2) + 2$

150. The senior team won 12 baseball games and lost 4. The percentage of games won was:
1. 25%   2. 66 2/3%   3. 33 1/3%   4. 80

KEY (CORRECT ANSWERS)

1.	4	31.	4	61.	4	91.	2	121.	2
2.	3	32.	1	62.	2	92.	4	122.	2
3.	1	33.	1	63.	2	93.	4	123.	2
4.	2	34.	2	64.	4	94.	3	124.	2
5.	4	35.	4	65.	1	95.	3	125.	4
6.	3	36.	2	66.	3	96.	3	126.	2
7.	2	37.	1	67.	3	97.	4	127.	2
8.	1	38.	2	68.	3	98.	2	128.	4
9.	3	39.	2	69.	4	99.	3	129.	3
10.	4	40.	3	70.	3	100.	3	130.	2
11.	1	41.	2	71.	4	101.	2	131.	2
12.	2	42.	2	72.	2	102.	3	132.	4
13.	1	43.	3	73.	2	103.	1	133.	4
14.	3	44.	4	74.	4	104.	1	134.	1
15.	4	45.	1	75.	2	105.	4	135.	3
16.	2	46.	3	76.	3	106.	2	136.	1
17.	3	47.	2	77.	3	107.	2	137.	1
18.	4	48.	2	78.	2	108.	2	138.	4
19.	4	49.	2	79.	1	109.	4	139.	2
20.	2	50.	4	80.	1	110.	3	140.	1
21.	1	51.	1	81.	2	111.	4	141.	3
22.	3	52.	3	82.	2	112.	1	142.	1
23.	1	53.	4	83.	1	113.	2	143.	2
24.	4	54.	1	84.	2	114.	1	144.	3
25.	4	55.	3	85.	3	115.	2	145.	4
26.	2	56.	2	86.	3	116.	4	146.	2
27.	2	57.	1	87.	2	117.	1	147.	4
28.	4	58.	2	88.	4	118.	2	148.	1
29.	4	59.	1	89.	4	119.	2	149.	3
30.	3	60.	2	90.	3	120.	3	150.	1

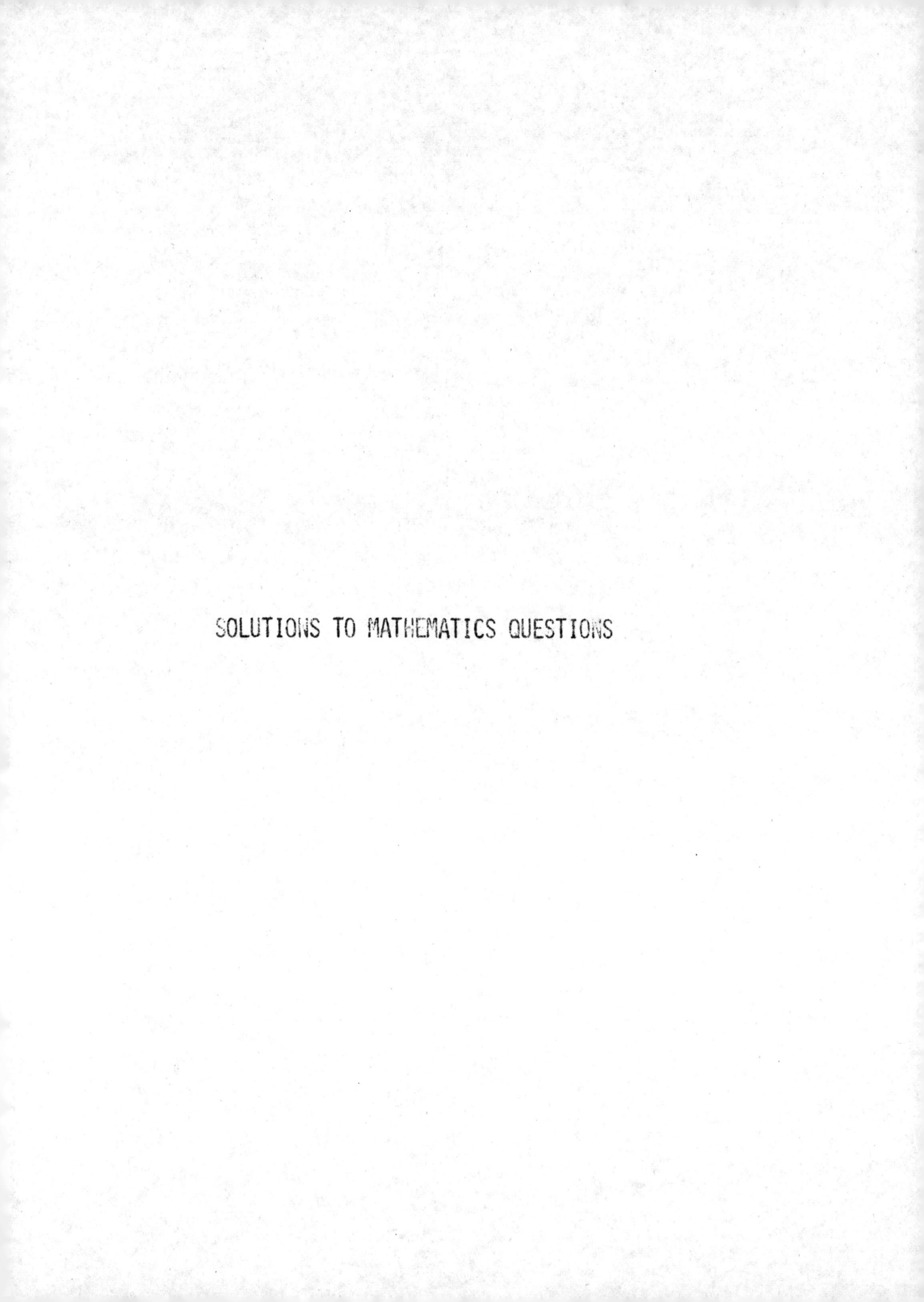

SOLUTIONS TO MATHEMATICS QUESTIONS

SOLUTIONS TO MATHEMATICS QUESTIONS

131. ANSWER: (2) 2' X 3'

   Finding dimension of width of closet

   $\dfrac{1/4" \text{ (plan width of closet)}}{9/8" \text{ (plan width of room)}} = 1/4 \times 8/9 = 2/9$

   ∴ 2/9 X 9' (actual width of room) = 2' (dimension of width of closet)

   Finding dimension of length of closet

   $\dfrac{3/8" \text{ (plan length of closet)}}{3/2" \text{ (plan length of room)}} = 3/8 \times 2/3 = 1/4$

   ∴ 1/4 X 12' (actual length of room) = 3' (dimension of length of closet)

132. ANSWER: (4) 8,100

   360' ÷ 4 = 90'

   90' X 90' = 8100 sq.ft.

133. ANSWER: (4) b/n

   By inspection.

   Average price = $\dfrac{\text{amount of money}}{\text{number of items}}$

   = b/n

134. ANSWER: (1) It is a geometric interpretation of the distributive law.

   The distributive principle in mathematics connotes a rule expressed by a distributive formula.

   Thus the diagram expresses geometrically the following relationship illustrative of the distributive law of multiplication:
   8 X 4 = 3 X 4 + 5 X 4

   32 = 12 + 20

135. ANSWER: (3) 120
   Let angle B = x
   Then angle A = 2x
   x + 2x = 180°
   3x = 180°
   x = 60°
   ∴ 2x = 120°

SOLUTIONS TO MATHEMATICS QUESTIONS

131. ANSWER: (a) 3' x 5'

Finding dimension of width of closet:

$$\frac{1/4 \text{ (plan width of closet)}}{5/8 \text{ (plan width of room)}} = 1/4 \times 8/5 = 2/5$$

∴ 2/5 x 9' (actual width of room) = 3' (dimension of width of closet)

Finding dimension of length of closet:

$$\frac{3/8 \text{ (plan length of closet)}}{3/2 \text{ (plan length of room)}} = 3/8 \times 2/3 = 1/4$$

∴ 1/4 x 12' (actual length of room) = 3' (dimension of length of closet)

132. ANSWER: (d) 8,100.

360° ÷ 4 = 90°.

90' x 90' = 8100 sq.ft.

133. ANSWER: (d) M/N

By induction.

$$\text{Average price} = \frac{\text{amount of money}}{\text{number of items}}$$

$$= M/N$$

134. ANSWER: (d) It is a geometric interpretation of the distributive law.

The distributive principle in mathematics embodies a rule expressed by a distributive formula.

Thus the diagram expresses geometrically the following relationship illustrative of the distributive law of multiplication.

b X 4 = a X 4 + b X 4

a: = 2: x 10

135. ANSWER: (b) 120

Let angle b = x.

Then angle A = 2x.

x + 2x = 180°

3x = 180°

x = 60°

∴ 2x = 120°

136. ANSWER: (1) $4x^2y^6$

$(2xy^3)^2 = 2xy^3 \times 2xy^3 = 4x^2y^6$

137. ANSWER: (1) $x^2 - 5x + 6 = 0$

The degree of an equation in one variable is the exponent of the highest power to which the variable is raised in that equation. A second-degree equation in one variable is one in which the variable is raised to the second power. A second-degree equation is often called a quadratic equation. The word quadratic is derived from the Latin word "quadratus," which means "squared." In a quadratic equation the term of highest degree is the squared term.

The roots are given as 2 and 3.
Substituting these values into equation

(1) $x^2 - 5x + 6 = 0$, we note that an identity results in each case, viz.:

Substituting $x = 2$

$2^2 - 5(2) + 6 = 0$
$4 - 10 + 6 = 0$
$0 = 0$

Substituting $x = 3$

$3^2 - 5(3) + 6 = 0$
$9 - 15 + 6 = 0$
$0 = 0$

This is not true for equations (2),(3),and (4).

138. ANSWER: (4) $[(2 + 3) \times 10] + [(1 \times 10) + 2]$
$25 + 36 = 61$
(1) $20 + 5 + 30 + 6 = 61$
(2) $50 + 11 \quad\quad\quad = 61$
(3) $20 + 5 + 30 + 6 = 61$
(4) $5 \times 10 + 10 + 2 = 62$

139. ANSWER: (2) one thousand

One thousand thousands = one million.

140. ANSWER: (1) three billion dollars

$10^9 = 1,000,000,000$

$\$3 \times 10^9 = \$3,000,000,000$

136. ANSWER: (1) $4x^2y^3$

$(2)xy^2 \times 2xy^3 = 2x^2y^5$

137. ANSWER: (1) $x^2 - 5x + 6 = 0$

The degree of an equation in one variable is the exponent of the highest power to which the variable is raised in that equation. A second-degree equation is one in which the variable is raised to the second power. A second-degree equation is often called a quadratic equation. The word quadratic is derived from the Latin word "quadratus," which means "squared." In a quadratic equation the term of highest degree is the squared term.

The roots are given as 2 and 3.
Substituting these values into equation

2) $x^2 - 4x + 3 = 0$, we note that an identity results in each case, viz.:

Substituting $x = 2$

$2^2 - 5(2) + 6 = 0$
$4 - 10 + 6 = 0$
$0 = 0$

Substituting $x = 3$

$3^2 - 5(3) + 6 = 0$
$9 - 15 + 6 = 0$
$0 = 0$

This is not true for equations (2),(3), and (4).

138. ANSWER: (1) $[(4 + 3) \times 10] + [(7 \times 1)] = 7^2$
$35 + 36 = 61$
(4) $20 + 5 + 24 + 6 = 61$
(2) $50 + 11 = 61$
(3) $20 + 5 + 30 + 6 = 61$
(5) $5 \times 10 + 10 + 1 = 6^2$

139. ANSWER: (2) one thousand

One thousand thousands = one million.

140. ANSWER: (1) three billion dollars

$10^9 = 1,000,000,000$

$3 \times 10^9 = 3,000,000,000$

141. ANSWER: (3) obtuse

   (1) An acute angle is an angle smaller than a right angle.
   (2) A right angle is an angle that is formed by one-quarter of a complete rotation (90°).
   (3) An obtuse angle is an angle that is greater than a right angle but less than a straight angle.
   (4) Scalene refers to a triangle which has sides and angles unequal.

142. ANSWER: (1) 83

   A COMPOSITE NUMBER is a product of two or more integers each greater than 1 (opposted to PRIME NUMBER).

143. ANSWER: (2) 4/5
   By inspection.
   (1) 3/4 = .75
   (2) 4/5 = .80
   (3) 2/3 = .667
   (4) 3/8 = .375

144. ANSWER: (3) 9/16
   6/8 = 3/4
   9/16 = 3/4

145. ANSWER: (4) $4.70

   $2.00 $2.00
   X 1.35   +2.70
   ─────   ─────
   1000 $4.70
    600
    200
   ─────
   $ 2.700

146. ANSWER: (2) $14,000

   Let x = total amount
   Then 1/2x + 1/4x + 1/5x = x - 700
   10/20x + 5/20x + 4/20x = x - 700
   19/20x = x - 700
   1/20x = 700
   x = $14,000

147. ANSWER: (4) 6
   By inspection

148. ANSWER: (2) .075
   By inspection

ANSWER: (3) $(1 \times 10^3) + (4 \times 10^2) + (9 \times 10^1) + 2$

$1 \times 10^3 = 1000$

$4 \times 10^2 = 400$

$9 \times 10^1 = 90$

$2 = 2$

1492

150. ANSWER: (1) 75

$12/16 = 3/4 = 75\%$

TEST 2

EXAMINATION

GENERAL PAPER

Questions 1-25.

DIRECTIONS: In each of the following groups, ONE sentence contains an underlined word which makes the sentence INCORRECT. Select this sentence and indicate your choice on the answer sheet.

1.
1. It was difficult to teach science to the local people, for superstition was <u>rampant</u> among them.
2. That his book may be a failure is a <u>contingency</u> that an author has to face.
3. To <u>assuage</u> his craving for cigarettes, modern man sometimes turns to sweets for satisfaction.
4. The early <u>rustication</u> of metal products has been a source of concern to industrial engineers.

2.
1. A man who holds an important executive position cannot afford to be <u>vacillating</u>.
2. The fire was completely <u>extenuated</u> only after the firemen had poured water on it for hours.
3. Doctors insist that any improvement caused by that drug is <u>transient</u> and that the patient receives no lasting benefit.
4. The <u>accretion</u> of many tiny organisms over a long period of time results in structures such as the coral reefs.

3.
1. Since there was no <u>dissenting</u> votes, the chairman declared the motion passed unanimously.
2. The League of Nations, weakened by the withdrawal of many member nations, soon became <u>defunct</u>.
3. Beethoven was undoubtedly one of the great <u>luminaries</u> of the musical world.
4. A <u>truncated</u> plant is one that grows large enough to have a woody stem.

4.
1. The <u>hiatus</u> is a gentle breeze which often blows in desert areas at night.
2. The experimenter concluded that the gain in achievement was not <u>commensurate</u> with the effort put forth by the teacher and the pupils.
3. Operation of this plan will be held in <u>abeyance</u> until necessary money is available.
4. The scientist insisted that the <u>spectral</u> image was the result of natural causes.

5.
1. Small round windows were installed in the basement lounge to carry out the <u>nautical</u> theme suggested by the interior decorator.
2. He needed a little time to <u>mull</u> over the details of the case before presenting it to the superintendent.

3. As it was only a <u>momentous</u> decision for the firm, he did not think it important enough for him to forego his golf game.
4. The author's prose had a <u>lyric</u> quality that suggested ability to create poetry as well.

6.
1. The rigid disciplinarian <u>derided</u> the efforts of her colleagues to maintain a democratic atmosphere in the classroom.
2. His tendency to play practical jokes was curbed after the distress occasioned by his latest <u>hoax</u>.
3. The cynical writer tried to belittle and <u>exonerate</u> every hero in our history.
4. His speed was <u>impeded</u> by the half-mile stretch of gravel road.

7.
1. The <u>acerbity</u> of his remarks convinced the audience that he was a philanthropist.
2. The unlucky petitioners were reduced to a state of hopeless <u>frustration</u>.
3. Through the <u>connivance</u> of the commanding officer, the prisoner was permitted to escape.
4. The prosecuting attorney demanded <u>tangible</u> evidence before instituting trial proceedings.

8.
1. An <u>astringent</u> has a binding or contracting effect on the tissues to which it is applied.
2. The <u>reclining</u> position seems natural for sleeping, but sentries have been known to sleep while standing.
3. She disliked having the children home for long holidays because they <u>mustered</u> up the house.
4. So great are his intelligence and learning that all of his writings are <u>imbued</u> with wisdom.

9.
1. The good teacher will attempt to discover <u>latent</u> talent in a pupil.
2. With care and attention to detail, he <u>manipulated</u> the clay until the figure of a deer took shape.
3. The garden party sparkled with the glitter of the varicolored <u>lampoons</u>.
4. The teacher pointed out the <u>fallacy</u> of the student's reasoning.

10.
1. With a new feeling of <u>respite</u>, the knight lunged forward to land a mortal blow.
2. The marathon racer needed no other <u>incentive</u> than the cheers of the crowd.
3. The <u>renascence</u> of an art depends on the appearance of new talent to project old ideals.
4. The popular hero actually found his greatest satisfaction in the admiration of a small <u>coterie</u> of intimate friends.

11. 1. The <u>felicity</u> of the author's style was matched only by the ingenuity of his plots.
    2. The award given to the talented young sculptor was one of the most <u>egregious</u> ever presented.
    3. Since the pieces of property were <u>contiguous</u>, it was only natural to consider single ownership.
    4. Many reforms have been introduced in the <u>liturgy</u> of the Church.

12. 1. The tellers prepared to undergo a <u>stringent</u> inspection at the hands of the bank examiner.
    2. A rabble rouser does not hesitate to <u>instigate</u> rebellion if it promises to serve his ends.
    3. As a result of his <u>vicissitudes</u> over his political enemies, Smith could now boast of an official car, a fine home, and a seat in the legislature.
    4. The team remained a contender for the pennant by virtue of a <u>tenacity</u> which even its most loyal adherents had hardly suspected.

13. 1. A <u>salient</u> feature of the medieval cathedral is the flying buttress, which gave stone the strength to reach heavenward.
    2. The forests of the West still carry incontrovertible evidence of their <u>pristine</u> glory.
    3. Under the protection of a Constituonal guarantee, the suspected racketeers thwarted their questioners with <u>impunity</u>.
    4. To provide <u>recreant</u> activity, the community center had a basketball court, a swimming pool, and a variety of games.

14. 1. It was her sole purpose in life to give <u>succor</u> to the victims of war.
    2. By bringing in additional members of the teaching staff, he was able to <u>adulterate</u> the class.
    3. A whole series of <u>seditious</u> acts took place before a state of emergency was declared.
    4. The demerits were <u>cumulative</u> and, as a result, he was eventually barred from participation in athletic competition.

15. 1. The huge furnaces were a primary instrument in the <u>temporizing</u> of the steel.
    2. Although often rebuffed, the nurse eventually won the <u>approbation</u> of her superior.
    3. To his friends' dismay, the general <u>dawdled</u> over his plans for the attack.
    4. The young lawyer's aversion to work led him to seek the most promising <u>sinecure</u> he could find.

16. 1. When he was home on furlough, Larry <u>regaled</u> us with humorous stories of army life.
    2. The enterprising young schemer was hoping to <u>proffer</u> by the mistakes of his competitors.

3. The receptionist at first ignored the visitor and then approached him with a <u>supercilious</u> air.
4. The clergyman often found it difficult to interest himself in purely <u>secular</u> affairs.

17.
1. Her <u>caustic</u> remarks about the latest fashions preceded her refusal to participate in the show.
2. The dean admitted that the young man had been expelled because of his <u>facetious</u> comments in the chapel.
3. Moved by the <u>pathos</u> of the occasion, the crowd broke out in unrestrained expressions of sorrow.
4. Because of his inability to reach decisions, Hamlet was often in a <u>redoubtable</u> state of mind.

18.
1. Generally regarded as being <u>fastidious</u> about his dress and person, the singer nevertheless espoused the current trend in unruly hair styling.
2. Because of the <u>chronic</u> nature of his ailment, the patient showed no alarm when the pain returned.
3. Do you know how <u>reprehensible</u> it is to steal from your neighbor or to blacken his name?
4. I am not at all <u>sanguinary</u> about the continuance of prosperous times in our debt-ridden economy.

19.
1. The unfortunate occurrences in Africa <u>portend</u> a long and difficult period of unrest and adjustment.
2. The achievements of our spacemen occupy a <u>superfluous</u> niche in the annals of American courage and ingenuity.
3. Although there was significant evidence of his <u>culpability</u>, the accused man showed no repentance or acceptance of guilt.
4. He asked no questions but voiced his criticisms in one <u>querulous</u> outburst after another.

20.
1. The young actor's efforts to express depth of feeling were so <u>ludicrous</u> that the enthusiastic audience responded with frequent applause.
2. The young man's attempts to display his <u>erudition</u> brought forth mocking smiles from his sophisticated listeners.
3. With a <u>lugubrious</u> air, the actor plunged into the rhetoric of the last tragic scene.
4. The strong walls and the high barred windows of the fortress <u>precluded</u> the possibility of escape.

21.
1. The <u>pirouette</u>, in which the performer whirls rapidly on her toes, is one of the common movements of the dance.
2. The speaker's use of numerous <u>circumlocutions</u> made possible his economical use of words.
3. The listeners were well aware of the <u>connotations</u> inherent in the dean's statement.
4. Relief from the storm was <u>transitory</u>; soon the driving rain began again.

22. 1. Some poisonous snakes are <u>indigenous</u> to the forests of the South.
    2. It was because of his <u>senility</u> that Grandfather Jones kept repeating the stories he had often told before.
    3. The dictator angered his countrymen with a <u>fatuous</u> display of his wealth.
    4. Through sheer industry and <u>indolence</u>, he rose to the top of his field.

23. 1. Being on the <u>leeward</u> side of the ocean liner, the small boats were relatively safe.
    2. In teaching, we must present problems that provide for <u>gradation</u> in difficulty from simple to complex.
    3. Many a man has worked hard all his life to amass wealth to be left to his <u>progenitors</u>.
    4. The breaking up of the ice in the rivers is a <u>precursor</u> of spring.

24. 1. Most people try to understand others' motives and do not <u>malign</u> people whose decisions seem unwise.
    2. The manager felt extremely discouraged when his accountant said that the business was becoming quite <u>lucrative</u>.
    3. When a member of the Peace Corps begins work, he must respect the <u>mores</u> and customs of the villagers, if he wishes to succeed.
    4. It is important to keep the moving parts of a machine well <u>lubricated</u>.

25. 1. His response to our direct questions were so vague and evasive that we suspected him of <u>duplicity</u>.
    2. In the long hall, with its low ceiling, the <u>reverberations</u> of the group discussions beat heavily against the ear.
    3. Because of his <u>temerity</u>, the child blushed, broke into tears, and left the room without saying a word.
    4. He had no friends, for people were alienated by the <u>virulent</u> invective that he addressed to everybody.

Questions 26-47.

DIRECTIONS: In each of the following groups of sentences, one of the four sentences is faulty in capitalization, punctuation, grammar, spelling, sentence structure, diction, etc. Select the INCORRECT sentence in each group and blacken the corresponding space on the answer sheet.

26. 1. I endorse the scholarship and service requirements for Arista candidates.
    2. The company was unprofitable because the officers could not establish effective laison between departments.
    3. I know whose books and equipment those are.
    4. The order has been given; consequently, you must acquiesce.

27. 1. The teacher, together with the entire faculty, were bound by parliamentary procedure.
    2. The doctor decided that there was a definite separation in the shoulder area.
    3. He reacted indignantly, like the man of principle that he really was.
    4. An exquisite piece of jewelry hung from her neck in an ostentatious display of wealth.

28. 1. The quantity of sugar lost must be small, for the bag still weighs almost five pounds.
    2. These three things I can swear to: the question I put to him, the answer he gave me, and the decision we reached.
    3. When the trial was over and everybody knew the verdict, an outcome that should have been obvious to anybody who heard the testimony.
    4. After all the speeches had been made, we came to the real business of the convention, voting for the candidates.

29. 1. The villagers suffered from the depredations of the enemy.
    2. These books are ours, but that one on the library table is hers.
    3. Mary will join with you and I in attempting to persuade the superintendent to repair the damage.
    4. The old man was careful not to deplete his strength.

30. 1. To receive a pupil's excuse for absence written illiterately on a piece of torn stationery is a shock to a beginning teacher.
    2. For one short week, the American tourists had a memorable vacation, fishing and swimming until they were exhausted.
    3. Wherever men may live, their life aims seem to be the same: to serve, to become rich, to become famous, etc.
    4. Being that he is still in high school, he needs several more years of education before he will be ready for any profession.

31. 1. His vociferous pleading made no impression upon the old judge.
    2. Only fear of reprisals restrained him.
    3. Where is the girl who he recommended?
    4. "The United States needs assurance by action--not words--that its citizens will be safe," was the official's reply.

32. 1. Using the opening line instead of the title, children often tell us that they are singing "My country, 'tis of thee."
    2. I must have read hundreds of novels, but this here book is the most exciting I have ever read.
    3. My only conclusion, after listening to hours of speeches, was this: not a single member of the club wanted to reveal his true convictions.
    4. That a man should remain silent is better than that he should tell a lie.

33.
1. English homonyms frequently confuse foreigners who are trying to learn our language.
2. That he failed to pass the test was no surprise to any of us.
3. By three o'clock I shall have either finished the work or call your office for further instructions.
4. Has he ever asked for special favors because he was once a professor here?

34.
1. I was embarrassed when the teacher singled me out for criticism.
2. He had to travel a mile farther than I.
3. More than any other prose form, drama relies on dialogue.
4. We must prepare for any emergency on our travels, whether they occur or not.

35.
1. If you are tired when you arrive home each day, you should lay down for a short time before dinner.
2. It was you, my friend, who encouraged me when I thought my property was irretrievably lost.
3. If any man here does not agree with me, he should set forth his own plan for ameliorating the conditions under which these people live.
4. The effects of a nuclear war may well be cataclysmic for all on earth.

36.
1. Jack is one of those boys who consistently rate high on standard achievement tests.
2. Using pseudonyms, the two editors have almost written every article in the magazine.
3. When the boys and girls went to Montauk Point, they took a picnic lunch.
4. Intramural athletic competitions drew large crowds from every class in the school.

37.
1. "Go back!" he shouted. "Its too dangerous here."
2. Not only the sales manager but also the salesmen were summoned to the president's office.
3. My brother informed me that he intended to accompany me to the public library.
4. Regardless of the consequences, he recommended leniency in this case.

38.
1. His study of Sanskrit grammar was both interesting and informative.
2. He is living in that village for the past four years.
3. There is strong support for the suggestion that all holidays be celebrated on Mondays.
4. The manager of the store asked why he had not been told about the robbery.

39. 1. Her gown was of heavy green brocade, and which was most becoming to her.
    2. "She said that you wanted to see me," said Louise.
    3. I wish he were more like Joe, an honor student in high school and a good athlete.
    4. The study of grammar can be an exciting experience when the proper technique of instruction is used.

40. 1. Although he was a true iconoclast, he often kept his thoughts to himself because he did not wish to hurt others' feelings.
    2. Many a boy learns that wanting to be a great athlete is quite different from actually becoming one.
    3. The chairman was disappointed because fewer persons were present than he had expected.
    4. "The train is due in fifteen minutes," said my friend, "we had better hurry or we'll miss it."

41. 1. There will be immediate increases in childrens' and adults' fares.
    2. Every one of the spectators held his breath momentarily.
    3. No two pictures in the exhibition were wholly dissimilar.
    4. Metaphorically, it is the tree of life-- the trunk, the branches, and the twigs.

42. 1. After waiting for two hours, the audience left the hall, angry and disillusioned because of the author's failure to appear.
    2. In spite of the expense, it seems likely that more American men and women will graduate college this year than ever before.
    3. If you study for the test, you may get a good mark; if you do not study, you may fail.
    4. If you do not know who owns the purse, let the usher keep it until the owner appears.

43. 1. Michael has been taking accordion lessons for more than two years.
    2. Betty and Sue, formed the nucleus of the group.
    3. The players complimented one another as they came off the field.
    4. The League of Women Voters published a fine analysis of the major issues confronting the voters.

44. 1. Throughout the day, we waited in the vicinity of the attorney's residence.
    2. My sister was overjoyed to receive the citation.
    3. After all his adventures, he seemed unable to settle down to a steady job.
    4. We asked uncle Tim to take us to the circus.

45. 1. Bob has an advantage over Al, for he knows the subject well.
    2. Give the parcel to whoever pays for it.
    3. Her husband is a carreer officer in the State Department.
    4. Regardless of our wishes in the matter, she intends to leave Saturday morning.

46. 1. By the time you arrive in London, we shall be in Europe for two weeks.
    2. The judge proceeded to overrule the prosecutor, regardless of all protests.
    3. Appearance, vitality, and intelligence -- these factors will be paramount in the contest.
    4. Trembling without cause may be a sign of emotional immaturity.

47. 1. In spite of the large number of plays in which he had appeared, he had had few successes.
    2. The morning was cold and gloomy; nevertheless, the boys insisted on going to the football game.
    3. When the test papers were returned, I learned that I had done well in all areas but one.
    4. Much snow had fallen during the night, the ground was white as far as one could see.

Questions 48-150.

DIRECTIONS: In each of the following, select the one of the four numbered choices which will make the sentence most nearly correct. On the answer sheet, blacken the space corresponding to your choice.

48. All of the following characters from Dickens are correctly paired with the novels in which they appear EXCEPT
    1. Sam Weller - THE OLD CURIOSITY SHOP
    2. Lucie Manette - A TALE OF TWO CITIES
    3. The Artful Dodger - OLIVER TWIST
    4. Micawber - DAVID COPPERFIELD

49. Among the following authors, the one NOT noted for his essays is 1. Charles Lamb   2. Robert Louis Stevenson
    3. Dante Gabriel Rossetti   4. Washington Irving

50. The author of TOM JONES also wrote all of the following novels EXCEPT 1. JOSEPH ANDREWS   2. AMELIA
    3. THE HISTORY OF JONATHAN WILD THE GREAT   4. PAMELA

51. The action in all of the following books takes place in the Civil War period EXCEPT
    1. GONE WITH THE WIND 2. DRUMS 3. ANDERSONVILLE
    4. THE RED BADGE OF COURAGE

52. The current musical play GOLDEN BOY is based on a play written by 1. Arthur Miller 2. Irwin Shaw 3. Clifford Odets
    4. Tennessee Williams

53. Ulysses has a series of adventures on his way home to
    1. Ithaca   2. Sparta 3. Troy 4. Rome

54. The literary world mourns the recent death of T.S.Eliot, Nobel Prize winner, writer of the lines
    1. This is the way the world ends,
       Not with a bang but a whimper
    2. Grow old along with me!
       The best is yet to be
    3. The world is too much with us' late and soon,
       Getting and spending, we lay waste our powers
    4. Much have I traveled in the realms of gold
       And many goodly states and kingdoms seen

55. Nielsen is a name most closely associated with
    1. a new approach to the Shakespeare-Bacon controversy
    2. publication of children's books
    3. literary criticism
    4. ratings of television programs

56. A biography entitled THE FOUNDING FATHER by Richard J. Whalen concerns the life of
    1. John Dewey 2. Charles Chaplin 3. Joseph P. Kennedy
    4. Oliver Wendell Holmes

57. The books entitled HERZOG, THE MAN, and THE RECTOR OF JUSTIN are all
    1. recent best-selling works of fiction
    2. biographies published within the past year
    3. novels written by one author, Saul Bellow
    4. works of non-fiction which deal with the three major religious faiths

58. POOR RICHARD'S ALMANAC was writen and published by
    1. Samuel Adams 2. James Madison 3. Richard Morrison
    4. Benjamin Franklin

59. Robert Frost wrote all of the following lines of poetry EXCEPT
    1. Good fences make good neighbors.
    2. Life has loveliness to sell.
    3. Home is the place where, when you have to go there,
       They have to take you in.
    4. Men work together ...
       Whether they work together or apart.

60. All of the following statements regarding Stephen Vincent Benet's short story, THE DEVIL AND DANIEL WEBSTER, are true EXCEPT
    1. The devil is known as Mr. Scratch.
    2. Miser Stevens tries to bribe Daniel Webster.
    3. Daniel Webster forces the devil to agree to stay out of New Hampshire forever after.
    4. A jury composed of demonic infamous Americans finds for the defendant, Jabez Stone.

61. Macbeth's tragic flaw can best be described as
    1. lust for power 2. inability to take action 3. jealousy
    4. blind patriotism

62. All of the following were contemporaries of Shakespeare EXCEPT
    1. Christopher Marlowe   2. Jonathan Swift
    3. Ben Jonson   4. Sir Walter Raleigh

63. D'Oyly Carte is a name associated with
    1. the Stratford festival   2. Dublin's Abbey Theatre
    3. Gilbert and Sullivan operettas
    4. a British school for training actors which is similar to our Actors' Studio

64. The "crime" in Dostoyevsky's CRIME AND PUNISHMENT is
    1. a plot to assassinate a leading figure of Russian nobility
    2. a methodical plan of vengeance taken by a political prisoner who fancies that the warden has treated him unfairly
    3. the deliberate murder of an old woman money-lender by a young student
    4. an intra-family rivalry in which members conspire to denounce one another to the government

65. Among the following, an example of the dramatic monologue is
    1. Bryant's THANATOPSIS   2. Browning's MY LAST DUCHESS
    3. Hood's ABOU BEN ADHEM
    4. Coleridge's RIME OF THE ANCIENT MARINER

66. The following quotations on death are all from the works of Shakespeare EXCEPT
    1. The heavens themselves blaze forth the death of princes.
    2. And all our yesterdays have lighted fools
       The way to dusty death.
    3. Fear death? -- to feel the fog in my throat.
    4. Cowards die many times before their deaths.

67. The raven repeats the word "Nevermore" in a poem by
    1. Henry Wadsworth Longfellow   2. Edgar Allan Poe
    3. John Greenleaf Whittier   4. James Russell Lowell

68. "If winter comes, can
    Spring be far behind?" is the conslusion of a poem by
    1. Lord Byron   2. Thomas Moore   3. John Keats
    4. Percy Bysshe Shelley

69. "My candle burns at both ends,
    It will not last the night;
    But, ah, my foes, and, oh, my friends --
    It gives a lovely light" is a quotation from a poem by
    1. Dorothy Parker   2. Elizabeth Coatsworth
    3. Emily Dickinson   4. Edna St. Vincent Millay

70. Each of the following presidents is correctly matched with a popular description of his administration EXCEPT
    1. Harry S. Truman - The Fair Deal
    2. Lyndon Johnson - The Great Society
    3. Theodore Roosevelt - The New Deal
    4. John F. Kennedy - The New Frontier

71. Republican proposals in December, 1964 for reapportioning New York State legislative districts led to charges by the Democrats of
    1. gerrymandering
    2. carpetbagging
    3. closed convenants
    4. closed-door policy

72. Each of the following statements regarding the development of the labor movement of the 19th century in the Western Hemisphere is correct EXCEPT
    1. The earliest unions were regarded as "conspiracies" and the labor leaders were often imprisoned.
    2. The philosophy of laissez faire then prevailing in many countries of western Europe and the United States helped promote the growth of unions.
    3. The democratization of voting rights to a growing number of unpropertied people gave an impetus to the growth of unions.
    4. The leaders of the labor movement were more interested in improving working conditions than in promoting revolution.

73. The basis for representation and voting power in the General Assembly of the United Nations is that
    1. each member nation is represented according to its population
    2. all member nations are entitled to equal representation
    3. representatives of the "Big Five" have votes that carry more weight than those cast by smaller nations
    4. charter member nations have the same numerical representation as, but more votes than, the newly admitted nations

74. All of the following were opponents of slavery EXCEPT
    1. John C. Calhoun
    2. William Lloyd Garrison
    3. Horace Greeley
    4. Ralph Waldo Emerson

75. Each of the following is an important advantage of the corporation as a form of business organization EXCEPT
    1. limited liability
    2. ability to raise capital through issuance of stocks and bonds
    3. continued corporation existence when one of the main owners dies
    4. combined ownership and management for efficiency in administration

76. Each of the following is considered an effective measure for farmers to use in soil conservation EXCEPT
    1. plowing furrows on slopes in straight up and down lines
    2. rotation of crops
    3. terracing of steep hillsides
    4. planting of trees on the sides of the fields from which the wind usually blows

77. Which one of the following statements about slavery in the United Statees of America is true?
    1. The original Constitution of the United States guaranteed the end of slavery.
    2. Crispus Attucks, a runaway slave, was one of the first Americans to die in the struggle of the American colonies against England.
    3. The United States of America was the first country in the world to abolish slavery.
    4. The Emancipation Proclamation freed all the slaves in the United States of America.

78. The statement below that best describes "Operation Bootstrap" in Puerto Rico is that it is characterized by
    1. determination to achieve complete independence from the United States
    2. attempts to secure additional funds from Washington, D.C.
    3. efforts to promote "tourism"
    4. general effort to promote all sectors of the Puerto Rican economy

79. All of the following are considered to be disadvantages resulting from commercial competition EXCEPT
    1. duplication of facilities   2. expensive advertising
    3. development of improved industrial methods
    4. unfair and destructive business practices

80. Each of the following geographic areas was acquired by the United States by purchase EXCEPT
    1. Louisiana   2. Florida   3. Oregon   4. Alaska

81. The multilateral nuclear force proposed by President Johnson to strengthen the military might of NATO has been most vigorously opposed by which one of the following?
    1. Great Britain   2. West Germany   3. Greece   4. France

82. Each of the following groups includes the names of three famous men whose contributions were made in a similar field of endeavor EXCEPT
    1. Galileo, Copernicus, Newton   2. Dante, Petrarch, Keats
    3. Titian, Raphael, Erasmus   4. Locke, Rousseau, Voltaire

83. The President's Cabinet, as a functioning entity, came into existence through
    1. an act of Congress   2. an amendment to the Constitution
    3. specific authorization in the original Constitution
    4. tradition

84. "Give me your tired, your poor,
    Your huddled masses yearning to be free," is an inscription to be found on the
    1. Statue of Liberty   2. Lincoln Memorial in Washington, D.C.
    3. Hull House of Chicago   4. Customs House on Ellis Island

85. "That government of the people, by the people, for the people, shall not perish from the earth" is a ...
    1. First ... 2. Gettysburg Address
    3. Emancipation Proclamation 4. Cooper Union Address

86. Of the following, the country which has not yet taken steps to permit its African colonial possessions to become independent is
    1. Belgium   2. Portugal   3. France   4. Great Britain

87. "A seaport that is a British Crown Colony and that has become a haven for refugees from Communist China" is a description which best fits which one of the following?
    1. Shanghai   2. Singapore   3. Hong Kong   4. Saigon

88. All of the following statements about Canada are true EXCEPT
    1. It imports great quantities of wheat.
    2. It is a member of the British Commonwealth, the UN and NATO.
    3. Many of its rivers flow northward and empty into Hudson Bay or the Arctic Ocean.
    4. It rates among the top three countries of the world in size.

89. Each of the following was a characteristic of feudalism at its height EXCEPT
    1. the manor
    2. a hierarchy of social and economic classes
    3. the growth of nationalism
    4. a system of protection and security for the common people

90. The Constitution of the United States of America denies to the states the power to
    1. levy taxes   2. establish schools   3. coin money
    4. make laws relating to health

91. Each of the following groups contains the names of men distinguished in the same field EXCEPT
    1. Carl Sandburg, Robert Frost, Edgar Lee Masters
    2. George Gershwin, Victor Herbert, Edward MacDowell
    3. Gilbert Stuart, Winslow Homer, Arthur Schlesinger
    4. John Dewey, William Kilpatrick, Henry Barnard

92. The head of the federal agency charged with the administration of the anti-poverty campaign of the government is
    1. Willard Wirtz   2. Sargent Shriver   3. Douglas Dillon
    4. Robert McNamara

93. Of the following, the one that gives the correct origin of the public metaphoric use of the term "iron country" is
    1. Franklin D. Roosevelt's summary of the Quebec Conference in 1943
    2. Winston Churchill's address at Westminster College in 1946
    3. Josef Stalin's terms of agreement with Churchill and Roosevelt at Yalta in 1945
    4. Nikita Khrushchev's first public address to the Russian People after the death of Stalin

94. The Supreme Court decision regarding the public accommodations section of the 1964 Civil Rights Law
    1. reemphasized the sanctity of private property
    2. made illegal the refusal of service anywhere in the United States
    3. made immune to prosecution anyone engaged in a "sit in"
    4. was based on the interstate commerce clause of the Constitution

95. In modern radio circuits a transistor is used to replace a
    1. resistor   2. vacuum tube   3. condenser   4. tuning coil

96. Of the following, the POOREST conductor of electricity is
    1. iron   2. steel   3. graphite   4. rubber

97. Of the following fibers, the one that is mostly protein is
    1. ramie   2. silk   3. sisal   4. linen

98. When water is decomposed by electricity, the two substances formed are
    1. hydrogen and oxygen   2. hydrogen and carbon
    3. nitrogen and oxygen   4. nitrogen and hydrogen

99. Of the following animals, the one which is NOT classified as a reptile is the
    1. turtle   2. frog   3. snake   4. alligator

100. Of the following, the one which does NOT illustrate the application of the lever principle is the use of a
    1. crowbar to dislodge rocks   2. nutcracker
    3. automobile jack handle   4. dolly to move a piano

101. Of the following, the one which is primarily responsible for the change of seasons is the
    1. rotation of the earth   2. sunspot activity
    3. tilt of the earth's axis   4. polar ice cap

102. Of the following elements, the one that is used to purify large masses of water is
    1. chlorine   2. iodine   3. sodium   4. lithium

103. The principal function of the red clood cell is to
    1. coagulate the blood   2. carry oxygen to the cells
    3. fight blood toxins   4. attack disease germs

104. Electrical currents are composed of moving particles called
    1. protons   2. neutrons   3. electrons   4. atoms

105. People in Australia cannot see the North Star because
    1. the sun's rays block the light from the North Star
    2. the earth revolves around the sun
    3. the earth rotates on its axis
    4. Australia is in the Southern Hemisphere

1. hydrogen and oxygen 3. halogen and argon

106. Automobile batteries are best filled with water which is
    1. aerated   2. chlorinated   3. chemically treated   4. distilled

107. The baby plant found in the seed is called the
    1. pollen   2. spore   3. egg   4. embryo

108. The Portuguese man-of-war is a
    1. jelly fish   2. flying fish   3. bird   4. crustacean

109. When heated, nearly all materials
    1. gain weight   2. lose energy   3. shrink   4. expand

110. Air that holds all the moisture it can at a given temperature is said to be
    1. precipitated   2. humidified   3. foggy   4. saturated

111. Food is preserved by refrigeration because cold
    1. helps to keep food crisp   2. helps to retain moisture
    3. retards the growth of bacteria   4. sterilizes the food

112. All of the following have been used successfully in the production of cancer in experiments on animals, EXCEPT
    1. viruses   2. tissue transplants   3. coal tar chemicals
    4. protozoa

113. All of the following are associated with hurricanes along our southeastern coast EXCEPT
    1. wind velocities of 75 miles per hour or more
    2. relative calm in the "eye" of the storm
    3. regeneration of intensity over water areas
    4. origin in the Bermuda High

114. Of the following, the one which is the best emulsifier is
    1. olive oil   2. soap   3. tincture of iodine   4. alcohol

115. Sir Christopher Wren, pride of the English Renaissance, distinguished himself as a(n)
    1. art critic   2. painter   3. architect   4. etcher

116. Among the following, the one who was NOT a famous cabinet-maker is
    1. Sheraton   2. Celline   3. Chippendale   4. Hepplewhite

117. Apron, flies, muslin, teaser, and flats are terms used in closest connection with which one of the following?
    1. blockprinting   2. advertising art   3. stagecraft
    4. mosaic work

118. "The Night Watch" was painted by
    1. Hals   2. Raphael   3. Titian   4. Rembrandt

119. Of the following sites of archeological research, the area found by Heinrich Schliemann and Sir Arthur Evans to yield their most important discoveries in art and architecture was
    1. Crete and other Aegean Islands 2. Mexico
    3. the temples at Saigon 4. Northern China

120. Copley, Stuart, and Peale are known as
    1. Colonial American artists 2. designers in modern glass
    3. English potters 4. English landscape painters

121. Jackson Pollock is best known as a
    1. modern architect 2. modern painter
    3. modern educator 4. costume designer

122. Of the following artists, the one whose life appears in a fictionized version in THE MOON AND SIXPENCE, by W. Somerset Maugham, was
    1. Van Gogh 2. Gauguin 3. Cezanne 4. Seurat

123. The romance of Rodolfo and Mimi is a prominent story thread in the opera
    1. LA BOHEME 2. LA TRAVIATA 3. THAIS 4. MANON

124. The standard string quartet employs all of the following instruments EXCEPT
    1. violin 2. viola 3. cello 4. bass viol

125. Marches are generally written in any of the following time signatures EXCEPT
    1. 4/4 2. 6/8 3. 2/4 4. 3/4

126. Of the following, the form which is most closely identified with counterpoint is the
    1. hymn 2. fugue 3. lied 4. nocturne

127. The "book" detailing the sequence of events in an opera is called the
    1. synopsis 2. resume 3. score 4. libretto

128. A humpbacked court jester is one of the central characters in the opera
    1. PAGLIACCI 2. MANON LESCAUT 3. RIGOLETTO
    4. PETER IBBETSON

129. The instrument for which Chopin wrote almost exclusively was the 1. harp 2. harpsichord 3. piano 4. organ

130. The American opera most recently premiered at the Metropolitan Opera House is
    1. THE KING'S HENCHMAN 2. PORGY AND BESS
    3. VANESSA 4. THE LAST SAVAGE

KEY (CORRECT ANSWERS)

1.	4	31.	3	61.	1	91.	3	121.	2
2.	2	32.	2	62.	2	92.	2	122.	2
3.	4	33.	3	63.	3	93.	2	123.	1
4.	1	34.	4	64.	3	94.	4	124.	4
5.	3	35.	1	65.	2	95.	2	125.	4
6.	3	36.	2	66.	3	96.	4	126.	2
7.	1	37.	1	67.	2	97.	2	127.	4
8.	3	38.	2	68.	4	98.	1	128.	3
9.	3	39.	1	69.	4	99.	2	129.	3
10.	1	40.	4	70.	3	100.	4	130.	4
11.	2	41.	1	71.	1	101.	3	131.	3
12.	3	42.	2	72.	2	102.	1	132.	2
13.	4	43.	2	73.	2	103.	2	133.	3
14.	2	44.	4	74.	1	104.	3	134.	2
15.	1	45.	1	75.	4	105.	4	135.	4
16.	2	46.	1	76.	1	106.	4	136.	4
17.	4	47.	4	77.	2	107.	4	137.	3
18.	4	48.	1	78.	4	108.	1	138.	4
19.	2	49.	3	79.	3	109.	4	139.	2
20.	1	50.	4	80.	3	110.	4	140.	4
21.	2	51.	2	81.	4	111.	3	141.	1
22.	4	52.	3	82.	3	112.	4	142.	3
23.	3	53.	1	83.	4	113.	4	143.	2
24.	2	54.	1	84.	1	114.	2	144.	3
25.	3	55.	4	85.	2	115.	3	145.	2
26.	2	56.	3	86.	2	116.	2	146.	4
27.	1	57.	1	87.	3	117.	3	147.	3
28.	3	58.	4	88.	1	118.	4	148.	2
29.	3	59.	2	89.	3	119.	1	149.	4
30.	4	60.	2	90.	3	120.	1	150.	2

SOLUTIONS TO MATHEMATICS QUESTIONS

SOLUTIONS TO MATHEMATICS QUESTIONS

131. ANSWER: (3) the associative principle

The sum of three or more addends is the same in whatever manner the addends are grouped.

Illustration

$$2 + 98 + 3 = 103$$
$$3 + 98 + 2 = 103$$
$$98 + 2 + 3 = 103$$

132. ANSWER: (2) 27, 160

$$2716 = 100\%$$
$$2716 \times 10 = 1000\%$$
$$2716 \times 10 = 27,160$$

133. ANSWER: (3) .640

By inspection.

134. ANSWER: (2) 1%

24 hours = 24 x 60' = 1440'

$$\frac{15}{1440} = 1440 \overline{)15.00} \quad .01$$
$$\underline{14\ 40}$$
$$60$$

135. ANSWER: (4) ordinal

Cardinal numbers are those used in counting: 1, 2, 50, etc.
Ordinal numbers are those indicating order and succession, as first, second third, etc.

136. ANSWER: (4) 62 1/2%

By inspection.
(Note: Set A - the two palms of a man's hand-equals 1 element or 1 set.)

137. ANSWER: (3) 4 ft. 9 in.

```
 16' 6"  =   15' 18"
-11' 9"     -11'  9"
             ‾‾‾‾‾‾‾
              4'  9"
```

SOLUTIONS TO MATHEMATICS QUESTIONS.

131. ANSWER: (3) the associative principle.

The sum of three or more addends is the same in whatever manner the addends are grouped.

Illustration

2 + 98 + 3 = 103
3 + 98 + 2 = 103
98 + 2 + 3 = 103

132. ANSWER: (2) 27, 160

27½ = 100%
27½ × 10 = 1000%
27½ × 10 = 27 . 160

133. ANSWER: (5) 649

By inspection.

134. ANSWER: (2) 1%

24 hours = 24 × 60 = 1440'

$$\frac{14.4}{1440} = 1440 \overline{)14.40}$$
$$\underline{14.40}$$
$$00$$

135. ANSWER: (4) ordinal

Ordinal numbers are those used in counting: 1, 2, 50, etc.
Ordinal numbers are those indicating order and succession, as first, second, third, etc.

136. ANSWER: (4) R: 1/2K

By inspection.
(Note: Set R = the two palms of a man's handsequals 1 element of 1 set.)

137. ANSWER: (3) 4 ft. 9 in.

16'6" = 15'18"
$$\underline{-11'9"}$$
$$4'9"$$

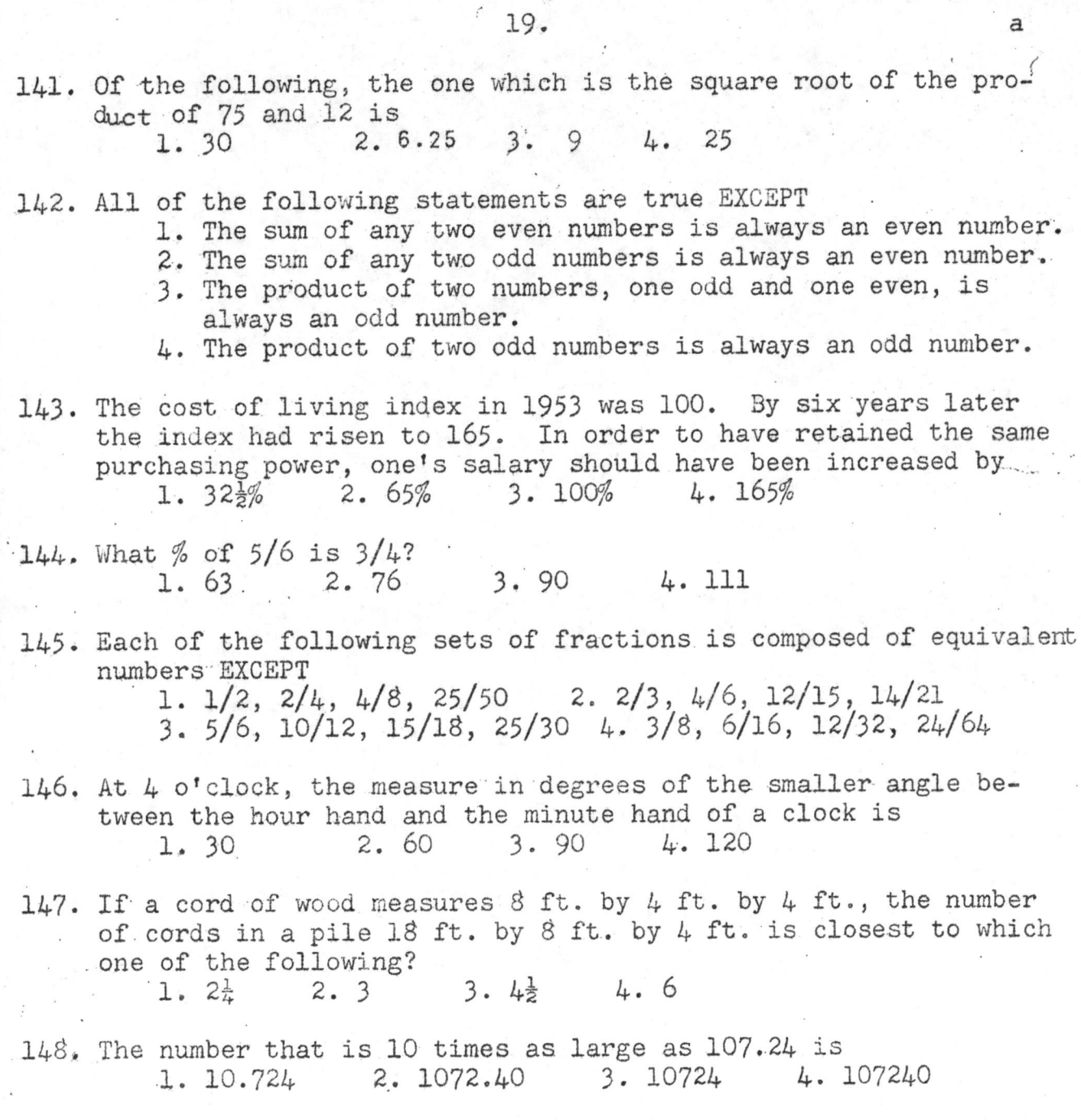

141. Of the following, the one which is the square root of the product of 75 and 12 is
   1. 30   2. 6.25   3. 9   4. 25

142. All of the following statements are true EXCEPT
   1. The sum of any two even numbers is always an even number.
   2. The sum of any two odd numbers is always an even number.
   3. The product of two numbers, one odd and one even, is always an odd number.
   4. The product of two odd numbers is always an odd number.

143. The cost of living index in 1953 was 100. By six years later the index had risen to 165. In order to have retained the same purchasing power, one's salary should have been increased by
   1. $32\frac{1}{2}$%   2. 65%   3. 100%   4. 165%

144. What % of 5/6 is 3/4?
   1. 63   2. 76   3. 90   4. 111

145. Each of the following sets of fractions is composed of equivalent numbers EXCEPT
   1. 1/2, 2/4, 4/8, 25/50   2. 2/3, 4/6, 12/15, 14/21
   3. 5/6, 10/12, 15/18, 25/30   4. 3/8, 6/16, 12/32, 24/64

146. At 4 o'clock, the measure in degrees of the smaller angle between the hour hand and the minute hand of a clock is
   1. 30   2. 60   3. 90   4. 120

147. If a cord of wood measures 8 ft. by 4 ft. by 4 ft., the number of cords in a pile 18 ft. by 8 ft. by 4 ft. is closest to which one of the following?
   1. $2\frac{1}{4}$ 2. 3   3. $4\frac{1}{2}$ 4. 6

148. The number that is 10 times as large as 107.24 is
   1. 10.724   2. 1072.40   3. 10724   4. 107240

149. A box 1 yard long, 15 inches wide, and 6 inches deep will contain how many cubic feet of air?
   1. 270   2. 90   3. $22\frac{1}{2}$ 4. 1 7/8

150. If a rectangle is 12 feet by $7\frac{1}{4}$ feet, its perimeter, in feet, is closest to which one of the following?
   1. 21   2. 38   3. 168   4. 148

131. In adding 98, 2, and 3, a child added the 2 to 98 before adding 3. This is an application of
    1. the distributive principle
    2. the commutative principle
    3. the associative principle
    4. none of these

132. If Y is 2716, then 1000% of Y is
    1. 2.716   2. 27,160   3. 271,600   4. 2,716,000

133. In which one of the following can the zero be removed without altering the value?
    1. 4360   2. 4.036   3. .640   4. 5.068

134. Frank spends 15 minutes every morning doing setting-up exercises. Which one of the following is closest to the portion of a complete day which this represents?
    1. $\frac{1}{2}$%   2. 1%   3. 10%   4. $62\frac{1}{2}$%

135. When the second game played in the World Series is mentioned, the number 2 is used in which one of the following senses?
    1. cardinal   2. associative   3. matching   4. ordinal

136. Let A represent the set whose elements are the two palms of a man's hands, B the set of 5 fingers on his left hand and C the set consisting of his left index finger. Then the union of sets A, B, and C
    1. represents the number 8   2. is equivalent to set A
    3. is a subset of set A   4. contains 7 elements

137. The difference between the two measurements, 16 ft. 6 in. and 11 ft. 9 in. is
    1. 5 ft. 3 in.   2. 4 ft. 11 in.   3. 4 ft. 9 in.
    4. 4 ft. 3 in.

138. All of the following statements are true EXCEPT
    1. Zero is the identity element for addition.
    2. In multiplication the number one may be referred to as the identity element.
    3. When zero is added to a given number the result is the given number.
    4. In the subtraction of whole numbers the identity element is one.

139. Each of the following sets of numbers is composed of prime numbers EXCEPT
    1. 2,3,5,7,11   2. 37,41,43,46,53
    3. 67,61,59,71,73   4. 13,17,19,89,97

140. All of the following are correct ways of expressing 4 x 25 EXCEPT
    1. (4x20) + (4x5)   2. (4x15) + (4x10)
    3. (2x25) + (2x25)   4. (2x5) + (2x5)

138. ANSWER: (4)

The identity element in subtraction, as in addition, is zero.
1 is the <u>multiplicative identity element</u> since the given number and the product are always <u>identical</u> when you use the multiplicative property of 1.

<u>Example</u>
1 x 3 = 3 x 1 = 3 illustrates the <u>multiplicative property</u> of 1: one times any given number equals the given number itself.

Likewise, 0 + 3 = 3 + 0 = 3 illustrates that the <u>additive identity element</u> is 0. The <u>additive property of 0</u> states that when 0 is added to any given number, the sum is the given number itself.

139. ANSWER: (2) 37, 41, 43, 46, 53

A prime number is a number which has no other factors than, or is divisible only by, itself and 1.
In item 2, 46 is not a prime number since it is divisible by 2.

140. ANSWER: (4) (2 x 5) + (2 x 5)

```
4 x 25 = 100              4 x 25 = 100
―――――――――――               ―――――――――――
2 x 5 = 10                2 x 5 = 10
2 x 5 = 10                2 x 5 = 10
        20                        20
```

141. ANSWER: (1) 30
75 x 12 = 900; the square root of 900 = 30

<u>Work</u>
```
    75
 x  12
 ―――――
   150
    75
 ―――――
   900
```

142. ANSWER: (3) The product of two numbers, one odd and one even, is always an odd number.
For example: 1 x 10 = 10

143. ANSWER: (2) 65%
By inspection.
(An index number is a percentage of 100%. An index number of 165 is 65% greater than one of 100.)

144. ANSWER: (3) 90

$$\frac{3}{4} \div \frac{5}{6} = \frac{3}{4} \times \frac{6}{5} = \frac{18}{20} = 90\%$$

145. ANSWER: (2) 2/3, 4/6, 12/15, 14/21
12/15 = 3/5
All the other fractions = 2/3

146. ANSWER: (4) 120

$$\frac{4}{12} = \frac{1}{3} \times 360° = 120°$$

147. ANSWER: (3) 4 1/2

18 x 8 x 4 = 576
8 x 4 x 4 = 128

$$128 \overline{)576.0} \quad \begin{array}{r} 4.5 \\ \underline{512} \\ 640 \\ \underline{640} \end{array}$$

Work
18
x 8
―――
144
x 4
―――
576

148. ANSWER: (2) 1072.40

By inspection.

149. ANSWER: (4) 1 7/8

$$3 \times \frac{15}{12} \times \frac{6}{12} =$$

$$3 \times \frac{5}{4} \times \frac{1}{2} =$$

$$\frac{15}{8} = 1\frac{7}{8}$$

150. ANSWER: (2) 38

12 x 2   = 24
$7\frac{1}{4} \times 2$ = $14\frac{1}{2}$
                ――――
                $38\frac{1}{2}$

TEST 3

EXAMINATION

GENERAL PAPER

Questions 1-25.
DIRECTIONS: In each of the following groups, *ONE* sentence contains an underlined word which makes the sentence *INCORRECT*. Select this sentence and indicate your choice on the answer sheet.

1.
1. She was injured so badly in the accident that the doctors were not sanguine about her survival.
2. Her meticulous habits made her well-equipped for the job of treasurer.
3. The colander slithered up to the little boy and struck him while his back was turned.
4. The parents were unable to cope with the boy's refractory behavior.

2.
1. The presence of a tannery is usually known because of the offensive odium emitted.
2. Thunder and lightning are often concomitants of severe wind storms.
3. Archeologists can reconstruct much of a civilization by examination of artifacts.
4. They could not proceed because they were told that the plans for the picnic were still nebulous.

3.
1. Astral patterns had always fascinated the astronomer.
2. When units of an organization do not communicate readily, there has been a failure of liaison.
3. The deciduous trees dropped a layer of leaves all over the park.
4. The engineers inspected the missile closely to see if the malfunction of the retinue had been caused by a short circuit.

4.
1. It was difficult for the newcomer to gain entry into the select cliché.
2. The prisoners were manacled to the wall and cruelly flagellated.
3. Although a waterfall may be frozen, there is probably never complete cessation of motion.
4. The way in which the detective stumbled across the stolen articles was completely adventitious.

5.
1. The timid newcomer circled on the periphery of the group of children.
2. Her moderate desires required only a modicum of the success for satisfaction.
3. The voluble contents of the closet made it difficult to close.
4. He was misled by her winsome manner and charm.

6.
1. The indulgent father balked when he had to meed out punishment to his son.
2. He gained his objective through chicanery and lost our respect.
3. The professor rejected the plan for the dissertation because of the amorphous outline and list of contents.
4. Encomiums were heaped upon the young violinist for his remarkable technique.

7. 1. The judge accused him of being an abettor of the confessed criminal.
    2. Her credulous nature made her easy prey to confidence schemes.
    3. They quaffed beer and told hilarious stories throughout the night.
    4. Because of their desire to salvage them, they decided to jettison the old automobiles in the junkyard.
8. 1. The emperor decided to assume the right of designating which son should succeed him, in spite of primogeniture.
    2. The three slaves had been bound and dentured to the plantation owner for over twenty years.
    3. When Whitman speaks of the "...splendid silent sun," he is utilizing an alliterative effect.
    4. He was a connoisseur of fine gems, having been born into a family of lapidaries.
9. 1. The mummers were so well costumed that the parade was deemed to be a huge success.
    2. Such nefarious deeds will lead only to international conflict.
    3. If you plan your diet carefully and forgo strenuous exercise, you may avoid another pleonasm.
    4. Complete silence reigned in the refectory as the monks had their evening meal.
10. 1. The child cast a furtive glance in the direction of the cooling pie.
    2. The principal discussed with the teachers the salient features of the directive.
    3. The denouement of the play comes when the knight arrives to rescue the fair lady.
    4. The matter was clear and inscrutable.
11. 1. As soon as he poured the oil into the aqueous solution, the separation of the liquids made him aware of his mistake.
    2. The diagnosis revealed that the lower part of the skull, just below the napery, had been damaged by the blow.
    3. The tremulous child stood before the class, fearful of beginning her report.
    4. The situation was exacerbated by the refusal of the two disputants to compromise.
12. 1. Smog over some of our largest cities has created a hazard to health of great concern to municipal governments
    2. The audience was grateful for the speaker's laconic style.
    3. The paeans revolted against the austerity of their conditions.
    4. The corporation's business activities were in a moribund state, a fact not known to the general stockholder.
13. 1. Widespread chaos, misery, and succor cannot provide a world climate in which our republic can prosper.
    2. Statements made under duress should not be admissible in a civilized court.
    3. He proclaimed that he was an agnostic, denying that man knew the final nature of things.
    4. The military police were alerted to watch for dissolute soldiers.

    3. The denouement of the play comes when the hungry matron by perjure the testimony.
    4. The batter was clean and immaculate.

14. 1. The actor's sepulchral tones chiled the audience.
    2. The lacuna is an animal extremely useful to the inhabitants of the Andes because of its ability to negotiate the difficult terrain.
    3. There was a recrudescence of drug addiction which proved alarming to the community.
    4. The physician had no recourse other than to prescribe a placebo for his neurotic patient.
15. 1. The teacher refused to accept minimal standards.
    2. Few persons are fooled by the specious claims of some modern advertisers.
    3. The onus of her misdeeds must rest on her own shoulders.
    4. The prisoners successfully dug an escape route and traveled through the subterfuge slowly and quietly.
16. 1. The grisly monster frightened all who saw his formidable appearance.
    2. That statement is an unconscionable lie!
    3. The group strained to hear the almost inaudible stentorian tones of the announcer.
    4. He would spend many hours reciting parables from the Bible.
17. 1. Instead of rising steadily, prices are oscillating between the current highs and lows.
    2. Her buoyant personality made her the most popular girl on the campus.
    3. The auditors accused the teller of collusion with the robbers.
    4. Her cutaneous remarks endeared her to the faculty.
18. 1. Because of his compulsion to eat between meals, the athlete became so orotund that he could not compete in any of the track events.
    2. That magazine is characterized by its eclecticism, giving both the conservative and the liberal viewpoints.
    3. Some educators are of the opinion that the matrix of a teacher's education lies in a thorough grounding in the English language.
    4. Tired of urban conditions, the authors decided to lead rustic lives by moving to cabins in the woods.
19. 1. A raconteur should be able to hold his listeners' attention to the very end of the story.
    2. The medieval castle contained a huge dudgeon.
    3. The explorers survived because they found supplies cached by an earlier expedition.
    4. Many experiences go into the development of a dour disposition.
20. 1. He seized the culprit by the scuff of the neck.
    2. In the interstices of the rock they found fossil evidence of marine life
    3. Because of the patient's stomach condition, the doctor ordered intravenous feeding.
    4. His denial was so obviously spurious that no one believed him.
21. 1. Edwards knew that he had riparian rights, and, therefore, decided to build a cottage on one of the banks of the river.
    2. He was the scion of a noble family which had migrated from Europe in the nineteenth century.

3. Seismologists agree that a fault in the earth caused the iconoclasm which reduced the village to rubble.
4. The calumnious accounts in the newspaper led him to believe that he should bring suit.

22. 1. Early buying by the public in the fall usually presages a good year for department store business.
2. The principal's secretary punctiliously followed the requirement that an appointment must be made before one could see him.
3. The spices in the sauce were so assiduous that few of the diners used the sauce at all.
4. He came to New York as an ingenuous country boy and remained to become one of the leading corporation lawyers of our time.

23. 1. His failure to see the value of the education he is receiving is a kind of myopia which is all too prevalent today.
2. To judge by their impassive expressions, the children were obviously delighted by the puppet show.
3. She was crestfallen to find that his love for her was but an ephemeral fancy.
4. The portmanteau was taken to the baggage room for storage during the ship's voyage.

24. 1. Any ornithologist should be able to recognize a brown thrasher or a nuthatch.
2. The restive horse refused to respond to his handlers.
3. The sumptuary meal was acclaimed by the dinner guests.
4. Because of rigid controls, the diamond market is never glutted.

25. 1. The study of any field involves ramifications not obvious to the beginner.
2. Diversity of customs would be lost if a country should decide to expatiate all persons of foreign origin.
3. His arguments show a lack of unity - even a dichotomy - in his thinking.
4. When the gale had spent its force, the sea gradually became placid again.

Questions 26-47.
DIRECTIONS: In each of the following groups of sentences, one of the four sentences is faulty in capitalization, punctuation, grammar, spelling, sentence structure, diction, etc. Select the *INCORRECT* sentence in each case and blacken the corresponding space on the answer sheet.

26. 1. The crowd was too excited to understand what the speaker was trying to tell them.
2. To whom did you give it to?
3. In the course of his dissertation, he made many allusions to Shaw's plays.
4. The venerable professor's opinions were often repeated by his younger colleagues.

27. 1. After this act, events moved rapidly toward a climax.
2. A treaty promoting American interests was signed.
3. The malefactor was quickly apprehended by the vigilant policeman.
4. Mary would neither take part herself in the production nor allowed her sister to do so.

1. Seismologists agree that a 4ault in the earth caused the
   commotion which reduced the village to rubble.
2. The calamitous accounts in the newspaper led him to believe
   that he should bring suit.
3. Early buying by the public in the fall usually presages
   a good year for department store business.
4. The principal's secretary punctiliously followed the requirement that an appointment must be made before one could
   see him.
5. The spices in the sauce were so assiduous that few of the
   diners used the sauce at all.
6. He came to New York as an ingenuous country boy and remained
   to become one of the leading connoisseurs=-lovers of our time.
7. It is piteous to see the value of the education he is receiving
   in a kind of myopia which is all too prevalent today.
8. To judge by their inaugural expressions, the children were
   obviously delighted by the puppet show.
9. She was desolate to find that his love for her was but an
   ephemeral fancy.
10. The paraphernalia was taken to the baggage room for storage
    during the ship's voyage.
11. Any ornithologist should be able to recognize a brown
    thrasher or a nuthatch.
12. The resting horse refused to respond to his handlers.
13. The sumptuary meal was acclaimed by the dinner guests.
14. Located in rigid controls, the diamond market is never
    stifled.
15. The study of any field involves ramifications not obvious
    to the beginner.
16. Dreams of currency would be lost if a country should decide
    to expatriate all persons of foreign origin.
17. His efforts show a lack of unity — even a dichotomy — in
    his thinking.
18. When the gale had spent its force, the sea gradually became
    placid again.

Exercise No. 7

Seventy in each of the following groups of sentences, one of the
four sentences is faulty in capitalization, punctuation,
grammar, spelling, sentence structure, diction, etc.
Select the INCORRECT sentence in each case and blacken
the corresponding space on the answer sheet.

16. 1. The crowd was too excited to understand what the speaker
    was trying to tell them.
2. 2. When did you give it up?
3. In the course of his dissertation, he made many allusions
   to Shakespeare's plays.
4. The venerable professor's opinions were often repeated by
   his younger colleagues.

27. 1. After this defeat, events moved rapidly toward a climax.
2. A newly promising American interests was signaled.
3. The malingerer was quickly apprehended by the vigilant
   policeman.
4. Who would chose to take part herself in the production
   of a jest designed to do so?

28. 1. The taxpayer declared that he is ready to discuss his return.
    2. We have but to say the word and we can have our every wish fulfilled.
    3. All his 7's looked like 1's; it was almost impossible to check his addition.
    4. In my opinion, no permanent solution will be effected by this dubious course of action.
29. 1. Much to his surprise, his classmates agreed to the proposal to cancel the picnic.
    2. Up to this moment the clergyman had not regarded himself as a predjudiced person.
    3. When he entered college he elected to specialize in Spanish history and advanced mathematics.
    4. There are fewer potatoes in the bag than I thought.
30. 1. The picture stood on the mantel, discolored, dusty, and forgotten.
    2. In the encyclopedia article it says that the tendency toward nationalism was clear by 1840.
    3. The miner could scarcely detect the gas emanating from the crevice.
    4. The horse that had won the race suddenly went limp and crumpled to the ground.
31. 1. The proverb, so short yet so meaningful, became the slogan of the marchers.
    2. "What is the value of across-the-board increases?" asked the fireman.
    3. The young performer picked up his mandolin, and strummed a tune.
    4. The next chapter treated of the causes of the American Revolution.
32. 1. Let us try to work this out together.
    2. Dinner over, he turned to his homework, eager to finish before bedtime.
    3. The court selected him as an intermediary because he was a disinterested party in the dispute.
    4. There was a law requiring a physical examination, and which made failure to comply a cause for dismissal.
33. 1. A picture of Martin Van Buren, who was not one of our better-known presidents, hangs on the rear wall of my room.
    2. My brother likes to go to New Hampshire with Uncle Bob to enjoy the winter sports.
    3. His work does not indicate the kind of perserverance needed if one is trying to obtain high marks.
    4. The speaker's habit of disparaging the achievements of great men showed him to be lacking in magnanimity.
34. 1. The children in the playground wondered whether the bell had rung.
    2. The children understand that the equator is an imaginery line.
    3. The questions were prepared with a view to studying the different strata of society.
    4. None of his pleas was successful in placating his father.
35. 1. Whatever his philosophy may be, his speeches do not reveal it.
    2. That he had swum the length of the lake in less than one hour was beyond our belief.
    3. By now, we know that this problem can never be solved.
    4. The result of the discussion was that we decided not to buy the car; which was just what I had advised at the beginning.

36.
1. If the police arrived earlier, there would not have been such confusion.
2. The New York City Parks Commissioner should provide closer surveillance of the parks in the city.
3. We came to a wide river, on the banks of which several rotted trees could be glimpsed.
4. Whether you like it or not, the lessons of history cannot be ignored.

37.
1. The helicopter stayed over my house for fully ten minutes.
2. It was my earnest desire that an accord may be reached.
3. The trio of sophomores looked good out on the court.
4. How many poets laureate have you known?

38.
1. Commissioner Simpson's speech instilled every listener with fresh confidence.
2. The new foreman tried to effect some changes in the established routines.
3. No one, not even the agents of the F.B.I., knows how many alien propagandists were working in the United States during WorldWar II.
4. His antagonist accused him of willfully concealing evidence.

39.
1. There were fewer persons present than the sale of tickets indicated.
2. Elected most often to be chief executive of the United States was president Franklin D. Roosevelt.
3. Each member of the team is expected to provide his own glove.
4. People who will not face reality use many euphemisms in their speech.

40.
1. To insult a famous man is far more serious than a nobody.
2. By throwing obstacles in the way of progress, a group can discredit itself.
3. One should never underestimate the loyalty of one's friends.
4. Our purpose, to put the matter bluntly, is dictated by necessity.

41.
1. The President made the White House a cultural center, but he also stepped up our armaments production as insurance against a suicidal war.
2. Should the new commissioner wish to bring about a change, he will have to institute a survey of current practices in the department.
3. His attitude will soon result in public censure.
4. Since oxygen is indispensible to human life, scientists are exploring the possibility of providing oxygen for future inhabitants of space stations.

42.
1. He could easily have won a scholarship if he would have devoted more time to his school work.
2. The new handbook supersedes all earlier bulletins.
3. It is a rare person who does not experience many vicissitudes in the course of his life.
4. The Reverend Arthur Williams will speak at the next meeting of the Writers' Club in the local high school.

43.
1. Ella's temperament will stand her in good stead not only as an actress but also as a musician.
2. Neither of us is eager to do the research.
3. Driving through the rain and fog, the Seminole reservation looked deserted.
4. Whatever they may think to the contrary, I do plan to attend the banquet on Veterans' Day.

44. 1. The General Organization must be a well-run school program; otherwise, its purpose is nullified.
    2. However you may look at it, the problem is a serious one.
    3. The charge, if supported by fact, is enough to send all of them to prison.
    4. To be guilty of an overt act, a definite action which can be shown to be what it really is, a crime against the state.
45. 1. The murderer failed to benifit from his crime.
    2. "My mother will be here," replied the little girl, "as soon as she finishes her shopping."
    3. Tired from so much walking, the girls asked permission to rest.
    4. A boy is really hundreds of different persons.
46. 1. Do you think that the data are helpful?
    2. I suggest that you send the document to the local library.
    3. Their comments being so indistinct, it's hard to say who's correct.
    4. They were happy to hear that the young piano student was liable to win the Tschaikovsky competition.
47. 1. The art expert agreed to examine the canvas which resulted in his decision that it was an original Van Gogh.
    2. Some distinguished scientists have alleged that a catastrophe is imminent.
    3. By the time you arrive, I shall have completed my solo.
    4. I wanted to apprehend not only the perpetrator of the crime but also his accomplices.

Questions 48-150.
DIRECTIONS: In each of the following, select the one of the four numbered choices which will make the sentence MOST NEARLY CORRECT. On the answer sheet blacken the space corresponding to your choice.

48. The author of IVANHOE and KENILWORTH wrote all of the following EXCEPT
    1. REDGAUNTLET   2. OUR MUTUAL FRIEND
    3. QUENTIN DURWARD   4. THE TALISMAN
49. The use of words in which sound suggests meaning is known as
    1. onomatopoeia   2. metonymy
    3. hyperbole   4. metaphor
50. Of the following poetic lines, the one written by John Keats is
    1. "She was a phantom of delight"
    2. "Hail to thee, blithe Spirit!"
    3. "Little Lamb, who made thee?"
    4. " A thing of beauty is a joy forever"
51. A man who sold his soul to the devil in return for his youth is the chief character in
    1. Molnar's THE GUARDSMAN
    2. Goethe's FAUST
    3. Shakespeare's THE WINTER'S TALE
    4. Moliere's LE MISANTHROPE
52. George Bernard Shaw wrote all of the following plays EXCEPT
    1. MAN AND SUPERMAN   2. CANDIDA
    3. THE DEVIL'S DISCIPLE 4. ELIZABETH THE QUEEN
53. The commander of the Greek hosts in the Trojan War was
    1. Menelaus   2. Agamemnon
    3. Odysseus   4. Stentor

54. All of the following recent best sellers are fiction EXCEPT
    1. THE SPY WHO CAME IN FROM THE COLD
    2. JULIAN
    3. CONVENTION
    4. THE INVISIBLE GOVERNMENT
55. William Inge is the author of all of the following plays EXCEPT
    1. OUR TOWN
    2. COME BACK, LITTLE SHEBA
    3. PICNIC
    4. THE DARK AT THE TOP OF THE STAIRS
56. Many followers of the adventures of secret agent James Bond are mourning the recent death of his creator,
    1. Agatha Christie   2. Ian Fleming
    3. Erle Stanley Gardner   4. G. K. Chesterton
57. The chief figure in Plato's dialogues is
    1. Aristotle 2. Sophocles 3. Creon 4. Socrates
58. Of the following, the posthumously published work of Ernest Hemingway is
    1. THE OLD MAN AND THE SEA
    2. TO HAVE AND HAVE NOT
    3. A MOVEABLE FEAST
    4. ACROSS THE RIVER AND INTO THE TREES
59. All of the following musical comedy stars are correctly paired with shows in which they starred EXCEPT
    1. Mary Martin - FUNNY GIRL
    2. Carol Channing - HELLO, DOLLY
    3. Carol Burnett - FADE OUT, FADE IN
    4. Beatrice Lillie - HIGH SPIRITS
60. In his ELEGY WRITTEN IN A COUNTRY CHURCHYARD, the poet Gray reflects that
    1. they also serve who only stand and wait
    2. a little learning is a dangerous thing
    3. we should gather rosebuds while we may
    4. many a flower is born to blush unseen
61. "As a beauty I'm not a great star,
    There are others more handsome by far,
    But my face, I don't mind it
    Because I'm behind it
    'Tis the people in front that I jar" illustrates the verse form named
    1. limerick 2. sonnet 3. ode 4. lay
62. Of the following, the author who wrote a biography of Queen Victoria is
    1. Esther Forbes   2. Paul De Kruif
    3. Lytton Strachey   4. Irving Stone
63. All of the following were daughters of King Lear EXCEPT
    1. Desdemona 2. Goneril 3. Regan 4. Cordelia
64. Macbeth meets death at the hands of
    1. Macduff   2. Lady Macbeth
    3. Banquo's Ghost   4. Fleance
65. An intimate account of life in 17th century England is found in
    1. More's Utopia   2. Wordsworth's poems
    3. Lamb's Essays   4. Pepys' Diary
66. The dramatis personae in a play consist of
    1. those characters who come to a tragic end
    2. the hero and the heroine
    3. all the characters
    4. the chief characters

67. THE STATUS SEEKERS and THE NAKED SOCIETY, which illuminate many of the customs and practices of our society, were written by
    1. J. D. Salinger
    2. Vance Packard
    3. Mortimer Adler
    4. Arthur Schlesinger, Jr.

68. "Loveliest of trees, the cherry now
    is hung with bloom along the bough,
    And stands about the woodland ride
    Wearing white for Eastertide" is a stanza of a poem written by
    1. Walter de La Mare
    2. Percy Bysshe Shelley
    3. A. E. Housman
    4. James Russell Lowell

69. "This above all: to thine own self be true" was advice given by
    1. the ghost to Banquo
    2. Lincoln to a bereaved mother
    3. Polonius to his son
    4. Franklin to his nephew

70. Each of the following is a major accomplishment of the Kennedy administration in the field of foreign affairs EXCEPT the
    1. signing of a nuclear test ban agreement with the Soviet Union
    2. establishment of an Alliance for Progress to aid in the economic reconstruction of Latin America
    3. renegotiation of the Panama Canal Treaty with Panama
    4. neutralization of Laos

71. The 88th Congress, which adjourned on October 3, 1964, enacted legislation dealing with all of the following EXCEPT
    1. civil rights
    2. health care for the aged under Social Security
    3. pay rises for Federal employees and officials
    4. tax reduction

72. The form of United States currency known as the Federal Reserve note was introduced so that
    1. there would no longer be any need for gold backing for our printed money
    2. the government would be able to borrow money at lower interest rates
    3. the supply of money would adjust more readily to changes in the public demand for cash
    4. the government could accept responsibility for insurance for bank deposits

73. Of the following, the country which best exemplifies a monsoon-type of climate is
    1. India   2. Japan   3. China   4. Korea

74. The International Date Line is closest to which ONE of the following?
    1. Japan
    2. Greenwich, England
    3. the Canary Islands
    4. the Aleutian Islands

75. The major purpose of the European Common Market is to
    1. foster political union among the member states
    2. bring about the gradual elimination of tariff barriers among the nation member states
    3. meet the economic challenge of the Soviet Union and its satellite
    4. make the group of nations belonging to it economically self-sufficient

76. Each of the following political heads of state is correctly matched with the country he leads EXCEPT
    1. Tshombe - the Republic of the Congo
    2. Shastri - India
    3. Macapagal - Philippines
    4. Nkrumah - Liberia
77. Jefferson's purpose in negotiating for the purchase of Louisiana was to
    1. prevent Spain from occupying the land west of the Mississippi
    2. secure an outlet to the sea for products of the western settlers
    3. prevent France from purchasing the territory
    4. end the controversy with Spain over boundaries
78. Of the following political practices and institutions, the one described in the federal Constitution is the
    1. organization of political parties
    2. appointment of members of the cabinet
    3. right of the Supreme Court to declare laws unconstitutional
    4. right of the president to veto laws
79. The United States is concerned with the problem of Cyprus primarily because
    1. it is causing dissension between its two important NATO allies
    2. it is an American naval base
    3. the Communists are interfering in the administration of the island
    4. the United States has invested huge sums of Marshall aid in this island
80. Each of the following is a result of the Civil War EXCEPT the
    1. rise of an American civil service system
    2. abolition of slavery
    3. inauguration of a new era of high tariff
    4. advent of the Solid South
81. Each of the following pairs correctly associates a patriot and his country EXCEPT
    1. Eduard Benes - Czechoslovakia
    2. Jose de San Martin - Chile
    3. Antonio de Santa Ana - Mexico
    4. Camillo de Cavour - Austria
82. All of the following have been winners of the Nobel Peace Prize EXCEPT
    1. Ralph J. Bunche   2. Martin Luther King
    3. Dwight D. Eisenhower   4. Albert Schweitzer
83. "No state shall make or enforce any law which shall abridge the privileges or immunities of citizens of the United States..." is a quotation from the
    1. federal Bill of Rights 2. Fourteenth Amendment
    3. Civil Rights Act of 1957 4. Declaration of Independence
84. The major purpose of the Ecumenical Council, as inaugurated by Pope John XXIII and continued by Pope Paul VI, is to
    1. modernize the position of the Roman Catholic Church on certain questions of ritual, theology, and canon law
    2. set up a new system of electing popes for the future
    3. denounce anti-Semitism
    4. bring about an immediate reunion of Protestants with the Catholic Church

4. advent of the "wild West"

85. All of the following were attempts at union among several colonies prior to the Revolution EXCEPT
    1. New England Confederation   2. Albany Convention
    3. Stamp Act Congress   4. Mayflower Compact
86. Bauxite is the ore from which we extract
    1. iron   2. aluminum   3. copper   4. nickel
87. "The great rule of conduct for us, in foreign relations, is... to have with them (Europe) as little political connection as possible" is a quotation from
    1. George Washington   2. Woodrow Wilson
    3. James Madison   4. John F. Kennedy
88. Of the following, the one which INCORRECTLY pairs an ancient civilization with a field of achievement is
    1. Babylonia - system of weights and measures
    2. Phoenicia - great engineering projects
    3. Greece - education as a preparation for living
    4. Egypt - a calendar of 360 days
89. The term, "hot line," refers to
    1. steps taken by the United Nations to meet the challenge of the "cold war"
    2. a cable laid on the ocean floor to improve interhemispheric communication
    3. a private communication system between the White House and the Kremlin to be used in any emergency which could result in war
    4. a tougher position to be taken by the United Saates in dealing with the Communist threat
90. The English Cabinet is responsible to the
    1. House of Commons   2. House of Lords
    3. reigning monarch   4. majority party in Parliament
91. Each of the following items matches a term frequently used in press dispatches with its correct meaning EXCEPT
    1. Vietcong - the anti-Communist guerrilla army of South Vietnam
    2. Aswan - a dam on the Egyptian Nile
    3. Ranger 7 - the first successful space vehicle launched by the United States to land on the moon on a photographic mission
    4. Telstar - the earth satellite used to improve intercontinental communication
92. The section of the United States which most vigorously and consistently demanded a policy of major internal improvements at federal expense before 1865 was the
    1. South   2. New England States
    3. West   4. North Atlantic States
93. Of the following, the greatest single export from Latin America in terms of money value today is
    1. petroleum   2. coffee   3. sugar   4. copper
94. Each of the following is included in the Civil Rights Act of 1964 EXCEPT
    1. the right of Negroes to access to all large-scale public accommodations, such as hotels, restaurants, buses, etc.
    2. the right of Negroes to register and vote on the same basis as whites
    3. the right of Negroes, in seeking job opportunities, to be free from discrimination on the part of employers and unions
    4. the right of Negroes to run for public office on the same basis as whites

95. In a balanced aquarium, all of the following are true EXCEPT that
    1. fish utilize oxygen dissolved in the water
    2. water in the tank should be completely changed daily
    3. snails, as scavengers, may help to purify the water
    4. in photosynthesis, plants use the carbon dioxide that fish give off in respiration
96. Of the following, the plant that is commonly grown from bulbs is the
    1. daffodil   2. geranium   3. petunia   4. fern
97. A recent book, SILENT SPRING by Rachel Carson, deals with the dangers inherent in the indiscriminate use of
    1. organic fertilizers   2. detergents
    3. pesticides   4. antiseptics
98. Of the following, the smallest units that determine hereditary factors, such as eye color, are
    1. chromosomes   2. vacuoles   3. genes   4. nuclei
99. All of the following are good conductors of electricity EXCEPT
    1. salt water   2. silver   3. carbon   4. glass
100. Of the following, the one that is the chemical formula for carbon dioxide is
    1. CO_2 2. C_2O 3. C_2O_2 4. CO

101. Of the following, the best procedure to follow in order to extinguish a fire resulting from the igniting of hot olive oil in a saucepan is to
    1. place a lid on the saucepan
    2. pour cold water on the fire
    3. pour hot water on the fire
    4. use a bellows to blast air against the fire
102. Of the following animals, the one that is most closely related to the hamster is the
    1. mink   2. weasel   3. chipmunk   4. skunk
103. Of the following birds, the one that swims under water to catch fish is the
    1. cormorant   2. herring gull
    3. sandpiper   4. black skimmer
104. Of the following, the one which is an instrument that measures wind velocity is the
    1. aneroid barometer   2. manometer
    3. anemometer   4. calorimeter
105. Each vitamin below is correctly paired with a food which is a good source of it EXCEPT
    1. vitamin A - carrots   2. vitamin B_1 - liver
    3. vitamin C - citrus fruits 4. vitamin D - yeast
106. The planet nearest to the earth is
    1. Mercury   2. Pluto   3. Venus   4. Jupiter
107. Many large rocks and boulders found in New York State parks are in their present locations chiefly because of the action of
    1. sedimentation   2. erosion   3. glaciers   4. weathering
108. A body that absorbs all colors of the light spectrum appears
    1. red   2. black   3. blue   4. white
109. Which one of the following results in the changing of edible oils into folid fats?
    1. emulsification   2. esterification
    3. hydrogenation   4. saponification

110. An acid secreted in the stomach of man is
    1. tartaric acid   2. hydrochloric acid
    3. ascorbic acid   4. citric acid
111. The metal covering of an ordinary dry cell is composed of
    1. aluminum 2. nickel 3. zinc 4. cobalt
112. With the aid of chlorophyll, light energy is converted into
    1. chemical energy   2. atomic energy
    3. nuclear energy   4. electrical energy
113. A cold front crossing New York State usually travels from
    1. north to south   2. east to west
    3. south to north   4. west to east
114. The sum total of the physical and chemical changes which take place in the body tissues is called
    1. metabolism 2. assimilation 3. digestion 4. osmosis
115. All of the following symphonies were written by Haydn EXCEPT
    1. FAREWELL 2. EROICA 3. SURPRISE 4. TOY
116. Among the following, the instrument which does NOT use a reed is the
    1. oboe 2. flute 3. bassoon 4. clarinet
117. Paul Henry Lang is best known in the music world as a
    1. conductor 2. singer 3. music critic 4. pianist
118. All of the following are violin virtuosi EXCEPT
    1. Mischa Elman   2. Yehudi Menuhin
    3. Cesare Siepi   4. David Oistrakh
119. All of the following are names of areas associated with summer music festivals EXCEPT
    1. Tanglewood 2. Interlaken 3. Chautauqua 4. Lancaster
120. The composer of MARCHE SLAVE also composed
    1. CAPRICCIO ESPAGNOL   2. FINLANDIA
    3. PICTURES AT AN EXHIBITION 4. OVERTURE, 1812
121. Each of the following noted musicians is correctly paired with the musical instrument with which he is usually associated EXCEPT
    1. Andres Segovia - guitar
    2. Artur Rubinstein - piano
    3. Pablo Casals - flute
    4. Isaac Stern - violin
122. All of the following are dance forms set to music EXCEPT the
    1. barcarolle 2. schottische 3. farandole 4. polka
123. The type of architecture that made use of gargoyles, spires, and flying buttresses was the
    1. Romanesque 2. Byzantine 3. Ionic 4. Gothic
124. The heart of the Italian Renaissance was in the city of
    1. Venice 2. Florence 3. Rome 4. Pisa
125. Among the following painters, the one best known for his romantic scenes of the sea and sunsets was
    1. Thomas Gainsborough   2. Jean Millet
    3. Joseph Turner   4. Pierre Auguste Renoir
126. Colors which have a common element and which are adjacent on the color wheel are called
    1. complementary colors   2. balanced colors
    3. rhythmic colors   4. analogous colors
127. The city plan of Washington, D. C. was devised by
    1. Sir Christopher Wren 2. Pierre L'Enfant
    3. Cass Gilbert   4. Gilbert Stuart

110. An acid present in the stomach is
1. nitric acid 2. hydrochloric acid
3. ascorbic acid 4. citric acid

111. The major constituent of an ordinary dry cell is composed of
1. granite 2. nickel 3. zinc 4. cobalt

112. With the aid of chlorophyll, light energy is converted into
1. chemical energy 2. atomic energy
3. nuclear energy 4. electrical energy

113. A cold front over greater New York brings about a flow from
1. north to south 2. east to west
3. south to north 4. west to east

114. The sum total of the physical and chemical changes which takes place in the body tissue is called
1. metabolism 2. dissimilation 3. digestion 4. osmosis

115. All of the following symphonies were written by Haydn EXCEPT
1. FAREWELL 2. EROICA 3. SURPRISE 4. TOY

116. Among the following, the instrument which does not use a reed is the
1. clarinet 2. bassoon 3. oboe 4. piano

117. Edward Grieg is best known in the music world as a
1. clarinet 2. flute 3. bassoon 4. oboe

118. All of the following are violin virtuosi EXCEPT
1. Fritz Kreisler 2. Yehudi Menuhin
3. Jascha Heifetz 4. David Oistrakh

119. All of the following are names of operas associated with former music festivals EXCEPT
1. Chanticleer 2. Intermezzo 3. Habanera 4. Barcarolle

120. The composer of MANON LESCAUT opera composed
1. CAPRICCIO ESPAGNOL 2. FINLANDIA
3. PICTURES AT AN EXHIBITION 4. OVERTURE 1812

121. Each of the following words instrument is correctly paired with the instrument with which it is associated EXCEPT
1. Andres Segovia – guitar
2. Artur Rubinstein – piano
3. Pablo Casals – cello
4. Isaac Stern – violin

122. All of the following are dance forms seen in music EXCEPT the
1. pavane 2. allemande 3. fandango 4. polka

123. The type of architecture that made use of flying buttresses, spires, and stained glass was the
1. Romanesque 2. Byzantine 3. Ionic 4. Gothic

124. The type of architecture that made use of the round arch was the
1. Romanesque 2. Byzantine 3. Ionic 4. Gothic

125. Among the following painters, the one best known for his romantic scenes was
1. Rome 2. Florence 3. Venice 4. Pisa

126. Colors which have a common element and which are adjacent on the color wheel are called
1. complementary colors 2. saturated colors
3. rhythmic colors 4. analogous colors

127. The city plan of Washington, D.C. was developed by
1. Sir Christopher Wren 2. Pierre L'Enfant
3. Cass Gilbert 4. Gilbert Stuart

128. A surface decoration made up of small pieces of glass or stone set in cement is called
    1. montage   2. majolica   3. mosaic   4. repoussé
129. Faience and stoneware are terms relating to
    1. lithography   2. embossing   3. pottery   4. architecture
130. All of the following painters were native Spaniards EXCEPT
    1. Joaquin Sorolla   2. Diego Velasquez
    3. Bartolomé Murillo   4. El Greco
131. The expenditures of a family for a certain month were as follows: food, $120; rent and operating expenses, $120; clothes, $60; recreation, $40; savings, $60. A circle graph depicting this information would show the expenditure for food represented by a sector whose central angle equals
    1. 90°   2. 108°   3. 120°   4. none of these
132. An employee receives $70 for a 40-hour week. Assuming a proportional deduction, the amount to be deducted for an absence of 2 hours and 12 minutes is
    1. $4.25   2. $4.05   3. $3.95   4. $3.85
133. John drove to his country home, a distance of 100 miles. He left the city at 10:45 A. M. and arrived at 1:15 P. M. His average rate (m.p.h.) was closest to which one of the following?
    1. 35   2. 40   3. 45   4. 60
134. If 0.8% of a certain steel alloy is manganese, the number of pounds of manganese in 2 tons of this steel is
    1. 32   2. 24   3. 4.6   4. 2.8
135. A salesman received $46.50 commission on a $300 sale. His rate of commission was
    1. 45%   2. 28%   3. 15 1/2%   4. 4.3%
136. 1 1/4 is what fraction of 7 1/2?
    1. 1/16   2. 3/7   3. 2/5   4. 1/6
137. When the principal is $600, the difference between simple interest at 4% per annum and interest compounded semi-annually at 4% per annum is
    1. $2.40   2. $.40   3. $.24   4. $.04
138. The difference between 2^5 and 5^2 is
    1. 70   2. 21   3. 7   4. 1
139. Of the following triangles, the lengths of whose sides are given, the one which is NOT a right triangle is
    1. 6,8,10   2. 8,10,12   3. 10,24,26   4. 18,24,30
140. If each number in a set of six numbers is increased by 2, the arithmetic mean is increased by
    1. 1/6   2. 2   3. 4   4. 8
141. The one of the following expressions that is NOT the equivalent of 8 1/3 per cent is
    1. .008 1/3   2. .08 1/3   3. 25/300   4. 8 1/3%
142. A man spent exactly 64 cents on 2-cent stamps and 5-cent stamps. Of the following, the one which could NOT have been the number of 5-cent stamps is
    1. 10   2. 7   3. 6   4. 4
143. The value of 2 1/3 ÷ 3/5 is
    1. 3 2/3   2. 3 8/9   3. 2 2/5   4. 1 4/9
144. If > means greater than and < means smaller than, which of the following is NOT true?
    1. 7/8 ÷ 5/6 > 1   2. 3/4 ÷ 8/9 < 1
    3. 1/3 ÷ 1/5 < 1   4. 1/2 ÷ 1/6 > 1

125. A surface decoration made up of small pieces of glass or stone set in cement is called
    1. mosaic   2. refolios   3. mosaic   4. repousse

126. Faience and stoneware are terms relating to
    1. lithography   2. embossing   3. pottery   4. architecture

127. All of the following painters were native Spaniards EXCEPT
    1. Joaquin Sorolla   2. Diego Velasquez
    3. Bartolome Murillo   4. El Greco

128. The expenditures of a family for a certain month were as follows: food, $120; rent and operating expenses, $120; clothes, $60; recreation, $40; savings, $60. A circle graph depicting this information would show the expenditure for food represented by a sector whose central angle equals
    1. 90°   2. 108°   3. 120°   4. none of these

129. An employee receives $70 for a 40-hour week. Assuming a proportional deduction, the amount to be deducted for an absence of 2 hours and 12 minutes is
    1. $4.25   2. $4.05   3. $3.95   4. $3.85

130. Jean drove to his country home, a distance of 108 miles. He left the city at 10:45 A.M. and arrived at 1:15 P.M. The average rate (m.p.h.) was closest to which one of the following:
    1. 35   2. 40   3. 45   4. 50

131. If 0.55 of a certain steel alloy is manganese, the number of pounds of manganese in 2 tons of this steel is
    1. 22   2. 55   3. 220   4. 2200

132. A salesman received $46.50 commission on a $186 sale. His rate of commission was
    1. .45   2. .258   3. .25 1/4   4. .25

133. 1 1/4 is what fraction of 7 1/2?
    1. 1/12   2. .17   3. .175   4. .145

134. When the principal is $840, the difference between simple interest at 4% per annum and interest compounded semi-annually at 4% per annum is
    1. $2.40   2. $3.40   3. $4.80   4. $5.76

135. The difference between 5% and 5 1/2 is
    1. .70   2. 3.21   3. 3.70   4. 7.1

136. Of the following triangles, the lengths of whose sides are given, the one which is NOT a right triangle is
    1. 6,8,10   2. 8,10,12   3. 10,24,26   4. 12,16,20

137. If each number in a set of six numbers is increased by 2, the arithmetic mean is increased by
    1. 1/6   2. 2   3. 4   4. 12

138. The one of the following expressions that is NOT the equivalent of 8 1/3 per cent is
    1. .083 1/3   2. .08 1/3   3. 25/300   4. 8 1/3%

139. A man spent exactly 94 cents on 2-cent stamps and 5-cent stamps. Of the following, the one which could NOT have been the number of 5-cent stamps is
    1. 10   2. 7   3. 8   4. 4

140. The value of 2 1/2 × 3 1/5 is
    1. 8 3/4   2. 3 8/9   3. 2 2/4   4. 1 4/5

141. If > means greater than and < means smaller than, which of the following is wrong?
    1. 7/16 + 5/6 > 1   2. 3/4 + 2/3 < 1
    3. 1/3 + 1/5 < 1   4. 1/2 + 1/4 > 4

145. The thrust in pounds of a jet engine is given by the formula
$$T = \frac{w}{g}(V_2 - V_1).$$
If $w = 64.4$, $g = 32.2$, $V_2 = 2000$, and $V_1 = 1000$, the thrust of the engine is

    1. 1000 pounds   2. 1500 pounds   3. 2000 pounds
    4. 10,000 pounds

146. A mortgage for $5000 on a house provides for quarterly payments of $250.00, plus interest on the unpaid balance at 4 1/2% per annum. The total second payment to be made is
    1. $344.03   2. $303.44
    3. $304.33   4. $333.04

147. If the least common multiple and the highest common factor of 14 and 35 are added together, the sum is
    1. 59   2. 63   3. 72   4. 77

148. The result of multiplication is called the
    1. product   2. multplicand
    3. ampersand   4. set

149. 7/8 is equivalent to all of the following EXCEPT
    1. .875   2. 8.75
    3. 87.5%   4. .87 1/2

150. The sum of the prime numbers between 20 and 30 is
    1. 26   2. 31
    3. 39   4. 52

KEY (CORRECT ANSWERS)

1.	3	31.	3	61.	1	91.	1	121.	3
2.	1	32.	4	62.	3	92.	3	122.	1
3.	4	33.	3	63.	1	93.	1	123.	4
4.	1	34.	2	64.	1	94.	4	124.	2
5.	3	35.	4	65.	4	95.	2	125.	3
6.	1	36.	1	66.	3	96.	1	126.	4
7.	4	37.	2	67.	2	97.	3	127.	2
8.	2	38.	1	68.	3	98.	3	128.	3
9.	3	39.	2	69.	3	99.	4	129.	3
10.	4	40.	1	70.	3	100.	1	130.	4
11.	2	41.	4	71.	2	101.	1	131.	2
12.	3	42.	1	72.	3	102.	3	132.	4
13.	1	43.	3	73.	1	103.	1	133.	2
14.	2	44.	4	74.	4	104.	3	134.	1
15.	4	45.	1	75.	2	105.	4	135.	3
16.	3	46.	4	76.	4	106.	3	136.	4
17.	4	47.	1	77.	2	107.	3	137.	3
18.	1	48.	2	78.	4	108.	2	138.	3
19.	2	49.	1	79.	1	109.	3	139.	2
20.	1	50.	4	80.	1	110.	2	140.	2
21.	3	51.	2	81.	4	111.	3	141.	1
22.	3	52.	4	82.	3	112.	1	142.	2
23.	2	53.	2	83.	2	113.	4	143.	2
24.	3	54.	4	84.	1	114.	1	144.	3
25.	2	55.	1	85.	4	115.	2	145.	3
26.	2	56.	2	86.	2	116.	2	146.	2
27.	4	57.	4	87.	1	117.	3	147.	4
28.	1	58.	3	88.	2	118.	3	148.	1
29.	2	59.	1	89.	3	119.	4	149.	2
30.	2	60.	4	90.	1	120.	4	150.	4

SOLUTIONS TO MATHEMATICS QUESTIONS

SOLUTIONS TO MATHEMATICS QUESTIONS

131. ANSWER: (2) 108°

    Food $ 120
    Rent, etc   120
    Clothes   60
    Recreation   40
    Savings   60
                $ 400 (total expenditures)

A circle = 360°

∴ $\frac{\$120 \text{ (food)}}{\$400 \text{ (total)}} \times 360° =$

    3/10 X 360° = 108°

132. ANSWER: (4) $3.85

2 hours and 12 minutes = 2 1/5 hours

∴ $\frac{2\ 1/5}{40} \times \$70 = \frac{11/5}{40} \times \$70 =$

11/5 X 1/40 X $70 = $770/200 = $3.85

133. ANSWER: (2) 40

From 10:45 A. M. to 1:15 P. M. = 2 1/2 hours

∴ 100 (miles) ÷ 2 1/2 (hours) = 40 (m.p.h.)

134. ANSWER: (1) 32

1 ton = 2000 pounds; 2 tons = 4000 pounds

0.8% = 0.008

∴ 4000 X 0.008 = 32

135. ANSWER: (3) 15 1/2%

$46.50 ÷ $300 = 15 1/2%   Work

```
         .155
   300/ 46.500
        300
        1650
        1500
         1500
         1500
```

136. ANSWER: (4) 1/6

   $1\ 1/4 \div 7\ 1/2 = 5/4 \div 15/2 =$

   $5/4 \times 2/15 = 1/6$

137. ANSWER: (3) $.24

   Simple interest per annum: $600 \times .04 = \$24.00$

   interest compounded semi-annually:
   (Step 1) $600 \times .02 = \$12.00$
   (Step 2) $612 \times .02 = \underline{\$12.24}$
   $\$24.24$ (annually)

   ∴ The difference is $.24

138. ANSWER: (3) 7

   $2^5 = 2 \times 2 \times 2 \times 2 \times 2 = 32$

   $5^2 = 5 \times 5 = \underline{25}$
   $ 7$ (difference)

139. ANSWER: (2) 8, 10, 12

   In a right triangle, $(\text{leg})^2 + (\text{leg})^2 = (\text{hypotenuse})^2$, or $a^2 + b^2 = c^2$.

   Item 2

   $8^2 + 10^2 = 12^2$
   $64 + 100 = 144$ (this is NOT a right triangle)

   Item 1

   $6^2 + 8^2 = 10^2$
   $36 + 64 = 100$ (this IS a right triangle)

   Item 3

   $10^2 + 24^2 = 26^2$
   $100 + 576 = 676$ (this IS a right triangle)

   Item 4

   $18^2 + 24^2 = 30^2$
   $324 + 576 = 900$ (this IS a right triangle)

140. ANSWER: (2) 2

The arithmetic mean or average is obtained by adding several quantities together and dividing the sum by the number of quantities.
Thus, let us assume that the set of six numbers consists of:
   1,3,5,7,9,11.
The sum of these numbers is 36.
The arithmetic mean or average of these numbers is, therefore,
   6 (36 ÷ 6),
Increasing each number by 2 would give us a sum of 48 (36 + 12).
The arithmetic mean or average of these numbers would be, then,
   8 (48 ÷ 6).
The arithmetic mean or average would have been increased, then, by 2.

141. ANSWER: (1) .008 1/3
By inspection.

8 1/3 per cent = (2) .08 1/3 or (3) 25/300 or (4) 8 1/3%.

8 1/3 per cent is *NOT* the equivalent of (1) .008 1/3.

142. ANSWER (2) 7

He must have bought an *EVEN* number of 5-cent stamps in order to spend exactly 64 cents on 2-cent stamps and 5-cent stamps.

Only item (2) 7 does *NOT* fulfill this condition.

143. ANSWER: (2) 3 8/9

2 1/3 ÷ 3/5 = 7/3 ÷ 3/5 = 7/3 X 5/3 = 35/9 = 3 8/9

144. ANSWER: (3) 1/3 ÷ 1/5 < 1

Item 3
 1/3 ÷ 1/5 = 1/3 X 5/1 = 5/3 = 1 2/3 < 1 (this item is *NOT* true)

Item 1
 7/8 ÷ 5/6 = 7/8 X 6/5 = 21/20 > 1 (this item *IS* true)

Item 2
 3/4 ÷ 8/9 = 3/4 X 9/8 = 27/32 > 1 (this item *IS* true)

Item 4
 1/2 ÷ 1/6 = 1/2 X 6/1 = 3 > 1 (this item *IS* true)

145. ANSWER: (3) 2000 pounds

$T = w/g \, (V_2 - V_1)$

$T = \dfrac{64.4}{32.2} (2000 - 1000)$

$= 2 (1000)$
$= 2000$

146. ANSWER: (2) $303.44

At the second quarterly payment there will be a balance of $4750.00
($5000 - $250).

$4750 X .045 (4 1/2% per annum) =
$ 213.75; dividing by 4 (for one quarter) = $53.4375 or $53.44

∴ $250 + $53.44 = $303.44 (total second payment)

147. ANSWER: (4) 77

A multiple is a number which contains another number without a remainder: e.g., 9 is a multiple of 3.
The least common multiple of 14 and 35 is 70.
A factor is one of two or more numbers, algebraic expressions, or the like, which when multiplied together produce a given product; a divisor: e.g., 6 and 3 are factors of 18.
The highest common factor of 14 and 35 is 7.
Therefore, 70 + 7 = 77.

148. ANSWER: (1) product

By inspection.

149. ANSWER: (2) 8.75

By inspection.

150. ANSWER: (4) 52

A prime number is a number which has no other factors than, or is divisible only by, itself and 1.
The prime numbers between 20 and 30 are: 23 and 29; the sum of these = 52.

EXAMINATION SECTION

TEST I

DIRECTIONS: Each question or incomplete statement is followed by several suggested answers or completions. Select the one that BEST answers the question or completes the statement.

1. If the curricular demands of a course of study prevent the teacher from using adequate time to go over the questions on a uniform examination, the *BEST* procedure of the following, would be for him to distribute review questions and
   1. answer papers and ask pupils to pick out questions for review at random
   2. make an analysis of frequency of errors on those done at home and review the questions most frequently missed first
   3. go over several questions each day over a period of weeks
   4. ask pupils to submit questions about their papers in writing and respond to a few of these each day
   5. model answers, together with scoring keys, which he drew up and used in marking their papers

2. Of the following, the *MOST* accurate statement regarding oral reports in junior high school classes is that they
   1. must be carefully supervised for form and content to be effective
   2. are worthwhile chiefly because they provide a change from the monotony of teacher domination
   3. are wasteful of time and provide learning neither for the speaker nor the audience
   4. should be prepared by pupils according to their own dictates to allow for maximum pupil expression
   5. should be extemporaneous and be used, wherever and whenever possible, in place of written reports

3. If a teacher is unsuccessful in eliciting the aim of a lesson through questioning in a few minutes, the *MOST* acceptable procedure, of the following, would be for the teacher to
   1. abandon the day's plan and reteach the previous day's work
   2. continue to rephrase pivotal questions to try to elicit the aim for as long as necessary
   3. state the aim and continue with the planned lesson
   4. give a homework assignment designed so as to help elicit the aim the next day
   5. lay this aside and take up the content of the lesson, knowing that the aim will be elicited from the students at an appropriate place in the lesson

4. Of the following, the *MOST* effective technique for determining whether a written homework assignment is clear is to
   1. examine in detail each of the assignments turned in the following day
   2. ask the class whether there are any questions about the assignment
   3. review intensively each of the directions in the assignment to make certain that these are understood

4. have pupils copy the assignment at the beginning of the period to see whether questions arise
   5. discuss the assignment with the class and ask specific questions to test understanding

5. The developmental lesson is *LEAST* characterized by which one of the following?
   1. medial and final summaries
   2. lecture and demonstration
   3. the eliciting of factual information through questioning
   4. the eliciting and clarification of an aim with the help of a motivating technique
   5. the movement of the recitation arrow from pupil→pupil, pupil→teacher, teacher→pupil

6. In distributing questions in a class of pupils of average ability, of the following, it is usually *BEST* to
   1. start with non-volunteers to develop their interest
   2. ignore non-volunteers
   3. call on volunteers principally until the lesson gains momentum
   4. ask pupils not to volunteer so that each pupil in the class will feel responsible for staying attentive
   5. answer yourself the questions that the volunteers cannot answer

7. Assuming there are three marking periods per term, which one of the following is the *BEST* approach in arriving at a grade for a student for the second marking period?
   1. Average all test marks of the student for that marking period and assign the multiple of 5 which is closest to this average as his grade.
   2. Average all test marks for each student and assign a grade to a particular student which will indicate his relative standing in the class according to these averages.
   3. Using test marks, class work, and homework as a guide, assign as his grade your estimate of the percentage of the work that has been presented that the student has mastered to date.
   4. Average all test marks of the student since the beginning of the term and assign the multiple of 5 which is closest to this average as his grade.
   5. Averaging test marks, class work, and homework on a weighted basis of 3, 2, and 1, respectively, assign the multiple of 5 which is closest to this average as his grade.

8. The teacher is informed by the parent of one of his pupils that the child will be absent for the next three weeks because of illness. Which one of the following is the *WISEST* course of action for the teacher to follow?
   1. Offer to visit the child frequently during his illness to help him keep up with the class.
   2. Offer to tutor the child privately after he recovers at a nominal fee.
   3. Recommend the services of another teacher who will tutor the child for a fee.
   4. Have one of the children in his class volunteer to visit the sick child each day and transmit the content of the day's lesson and the assignment to him.

5. Prepare an adequate number of written and study assignments for the child to do during his absence to minimize the effect of the loss of classroom instruction.

9. Which one of the following methods for preventing cheating on tests is MOST effective?
    1. Mention several methods students use in cheating and warn the class that you will be watching carefully for them.
    2. Prepare two separate tests for alternate rows.
    3. Watch the class carefully and very severely punish the first offender to set an example for the rest.
    4. Call on the services of several Arista members to assist you in proctoring the test.
    5. Directly in front of the class, warn one of the students, whom you suspect to be a ringleader, that you will not tolerate cheating of any kind.

10. A test is considered reliable if it
    1. measures what it is intended to measure
    2. predicts future behavior
    3. shows consistent growth from previous achievement test scores
    4. measures something consistently
    5. can be counted on to distinguish between the bright, the average, and the slow students

11. Of the following, the one statement that is GENERALLY true of the slow learner is that he is
    1. slow in forming associations between words and ideas
    2. poor in reading but good in arithmetic
    3. more likely to develop into a delinquent
    4. in respect to the general population, at or about the 90th percentile in mechanical ability
    5. more capable of nonverbal reasoning than verbal reasoning

12. In day to day practice, the BEST procedure for handling medial summaries of a lesson is that they be
    1. stated briefly by the teacher
    2. developed into blackboard outlines
    3. elicited from students
    4. be given at the middle of the lesson
    5. developed into mimeographed sheets and be retained in a loose leaf binder

13. Of the following, probably the BEST way for the teacher to determine the true ability of a student is to
    1. consult frankly with his parents
    2. use a carefully standardized group intelligence test with age-grade equivalents
    3. review his records, observe him very carefully and analyze his performance
    4. gain the confidence of a physician who has served the family for years
    5. send him to a college psychological testing center and have him take the full complement of tests

14. Of the following, the BEST basis for determining students' grades is usually
    1. tests only
    2. tests, homework, and class participation

3. tests, homework, class participation, and conduct
4. tests and class participation
5. general estimate, based on their most recent and most successful performances

15. Of the following, the one MOST characteristic of the normally developing adolescent is
    1. continuous need for parental support
    2. development of emotional maturity
    3. desire for constant domination by siblings
    4. freedom from peer group identification
    5. emphasis on expression of individuality and independence

16. Assuming that a student asks a question which the teacher cannot immediately answer, the BEST way, among the following, for the teacher to handle the situation is to
    1. attempt to answer the question anyway
    2. admit he does not know and have the answer looked up and reported to the class at the same or next lesson
    3. state that the question will be answered at a future time
    4. accept the answer of a student who seems to know
    5. ignore the question as though he did not hear it, but then, later on, after finding the answer, refer incidentally to the question and give the answer

17. Of the following, the LEAST effective method for obtaining pupil participation is to
    1. permit pupils to volunteer to answer
    2. permit pupils to evaluate each others' answers
    3. permit pupils to help develop the wording of the aim of the lesson
    4. use the experiences of pupils in the lesson development
    5. permit pupils to answer in concert

18. Of the following, the record data MOST likely to indicate a slow learner would show that the pupil has
    1. repeated failure in mathematics
    2. a mental age considerably higher than the chronological age
    3. reading achievement at the 20th percentile
    4. been an only child of divorced parents
    5. a poor handwriting index

19. Group morale will be higher, as a rule, in classes that are run in which one of the following patterns?
    1. democratic   2. laissez-faire   3. authoritarian
    4. individual   5. pupil-teacher

20. Of the following, the LEAST desirable procedure for the assignment of project work is that it should
    1. be requested by the student
    2. provide for teacher conferences with pupils
    3. be given only to superior or gifted students
    4. be a substitute for the daily requirements of the course
    5. take the place of homework

21. The *LEAST* acceptable of the following procedures for using test scores on teacher-made periodic tests is to
    1. prepare a chart or graph so that each pupil's marks are posted on the bulletin board
    2. train each pupil to keep an individual test score graph in his own note book
    3. mount only perfect papers on the bulletin boards
    4. train each pupil to keep a folder of his own corrected test papers
    5. group children in committees

22. Of the following, the *BEST* reason for parent-teacher interviews is that the teacher
    1. be enabled to communicate the importance of homework
    2. and the parent share the task of motivating the student
    3. be enabled to advise the parent about the child's needs
    4. be enabled to tell the parent about the child's strength
    5. may be enabled to explain the current philosophy of education, together with principles and practices, of the school

23. A good motivation for a class is always intended to accomplish all of the following *EXCEPT*
    1. develop a sustained drive
    2. create the feeling of an unsolved problem
    3. communicate the information basic to the lesson to be taught
    4. develop around needs of the adolescent
    5. refer to previous learnings or lessons

24. Which one of the following approaches to the teaching of democratic attitudes is the *LEAST* effective?
    1. Attitudes should be caught rather than taught
    2. The learner should identify himself with outstanding democratic leaders
    3. Direct teaching of moral values will be most productive
    4. Experiences in democratic living will develop proper democratic attitudes
    5. Participation in civic affairs shows democracy at work

25. Which one of the following basic suggestions should one carry out *FIRST* to establish good class management?
    1. Train the class in distribution of material
    2. Discuss the aims of the year's work
    3. Make out a seating plan
    4. Survey the work of the semester
    5. Discuss the required rules for proper class behavior

26. Of the following, the *MOST* important element in a problem situation in terms of the pupil's learning is that
    1. the pupil must feel a need or desire to find a solution
    2. the problem situation must come from the experiences of the pupil
    3. there should not be a barrier between the pupil and the solution
    4. the problem should be clear cut and solvable in only one way
    5. there should be a reward for finding the correct solution

27. Which one of the following is GENERALLY a sound principle of questioning for the teacher to follow?
    1. Speak very loudly to make sure all pupils hear you, especially those who are inattentive
    2. Repeat pupils' answers to make sure all pupils have heard them
    3. Distribute questions widely so that all or nearly all pupils have a chance to participate
    4. Encourage chorus responses so that the teacher will know how many pupils know the answer
    5. Call only upon those who volunteer lest you hurt the feelings of non-volunteers by calling upon them and having them make a spectacle of themselves in front of the whole class

28. A good junior high school lesson will frequently employ which one of the following as its initial phase?
    1. detailed correction of all parts of the previous night's homework
    2. explanation of a new kind of problem by the teacher
    3. warm-up drill for pupils
    4. "sitting up tall" for extra credit
    5. good joke with a double entendre

29. Which one of the following descriptions of routines is LEAST indicative of good classroom management?
    1. Initiating distribution of paper by pupil monitor's placing a pile on first desk of each row
    2. Adjusting of windows and shades by a pupil monitor
    3. Placing a sampling of homework examples on chalk board for correction and discussion
    4. Having students choose seats and then preparing a seating plan for each class
    5. Having a pupil monitor check attendance in your Delaney Book

30. Which one of the following is a correct statement concerning the administration of a pre-test?
    1. It unnecessarily consumes time to acquire information more readily discovered by the teacher by informal means.
    2. It should be confined to the beginning of the school year for the entire grade.
    3. It dispenses with the need for review.
    4. A pre-test is usually given only at the inception of a unit of several weeks' duration.
    5. It serves in part as a survey of individual and class background and readiness.

31. Which one of the following is an INCORRECT procedure in constructing a multiple-choice, short-answer test?
    1. Providing a separate answer sheet, particularly for a long test
    2. Placing a number of easy questions at the beginning of the test
    3. Insuring that correct choices are not obvious
    4. Arranging correct answers according to a pattern
    5. Providing for gradation of difficulty in the sequence of presentation of questions

32. Which one of the following is generally the LEAST effective method of informing pupils of homework assignments?
    1. dictation of assignments by teacher
    2. distribution of duplicated assignment sheets
    3. recording on chalk board by the teacher before period begins
    4. recording on chalk board by pupil at the beginning of lesson
    5. making a different student responsible each day for recording the assignment on the chalk board

33. Of the following, the BEST technique in following up homework is:
    1. The homework should be marked as a test daily
    2. Several students should place their homework on the chalk board daily
    3. Very little, if any, class time should be consumed in going over homework
    4. Only those exercises and problems with which pupils have difficulty should normally be explained
    5. A monitor in each row should check the homework daily

34. Which one of the following is the LEAST valid method of evaluating a pupil's understanding and readiness for advanced work?
    1. Asking the parent how long the pupil takes to do homework assignments
    2. Observing the pupil as he works on practice material in class
    3. Listening to the pupil's explanation of how he arrived at an answer
    4. Analyzing the pupil's test papers
    5. Examining the pupil's responses as an individual and as a group member

35. When a parent keeps an appointment to visit a teacher to complain about the progress of her child, the teacher may properly do which one of the following?
    1. Tell the parent that many children in the class are failing
    2. Ask the parent whether she has carefully supervised her child's homework
    3. Be fully prepared for the interview by carefully studying the pupil's complete school record
    4. Point out that the pupil was probably not held to a high standard in previous grades
    5. Inform the parent that she's lucky that her child has not been kicked out or suspended up to this time

36. Which one of the following is usually a pedagogically UNSOUND procedure in utilizing a filmstrip with a junior high school class?
    1. Including a follow-up related to the filmstrip in the home study assignment
    2. Employing the filmstrip as a review device
    3. Having pupils read and explain the captions
    4. Showing a complete filmstrip of 47 frames in one period
    5. Asking three or more pithy questions relating the filmstrip to the ongoing unit

37. Of the following possible techniques for use in connection with audio-visual aids, the BEST is for the
    1. students to take notes during the showing of a film
    2. teacher to explain the film during its showing
    3. teacher to make auxiliary use of the chalk board during the showing of the film
    4. teacher to stop the film at certain crucial points to emphasize important knowledges or skills
    5. class to observe the film without interruption and be questioned about it thereafter

38. Of the following, which one represents the LEAST effective disciplinary technique?
    1. Compelling pupils under threat of punishment to observe class rules
    2. Helping pupils to enjoy classwork through the use of meaningful activities
    3. Providing wide participation for all pupils in the work and administration of the class
    4. Discouraging lateness to class by starting each period with an interesting activity
    5. Having the homework assignment and/or two or three motivating questions on the board as the class enters the room

39. Which one of the following is a GOOD practical procedure for a teacher to utilize in maintaining discipline?
    1. Learn the names of all pupils as quickly as possible at the beginning of the year
    2. Disregard most minor infractions to avoid magnifying their importance
    3. Prepare a list designating punishments for various infractions and follow it rigidly
    4. Avoid displaying a sense of humor during the first few weeks of the term
    5. Maintain a posture of strictness and rigidity for the first third of the term

40. The ratio between the measure of the pupil's actual mental maturity and that which is normal for one of his chronological age is known as the pupil's
    1. E.Q.   2. I.Q.   3. A.Q.   4. M.A.   5. R.G.

41. Of the following, the LEAST desirable technique in performing a demonstration is for
    1. the teacher to accompany the demonstration with a detailed commentary
    2. the apparatus used to be on a large scale
    3. the apparatus to be pre-tested
    4. the teacher to rehearse the demonstration so that he can perform it easily and smoothly
    5. the teacher to have at hand all the apparatus needed for the experiment before he begins his demonstration

42. Learning is MOST apt to happen when the
    1. pupil understands the importance of what he is doing
    2. pupil is told all the necessary facts by a knowledgeable teacher
    3. pupil handles things
    4. academic standards of the school are kept high
    5. standards of discipline are high and firmly enforced

43. Of the following, the one MOST serious objection to laboratory lessons, as they are usually conducted, is that
    1. many of the activities are unsafe for unskilled pupils
    2. there is little opportunity for creativity and solving of problems
    3. there is usually insufficient apparatus for individual work by pupils
    4. most of the experiments cannot be performed in a 40-minute laboratory period
    5. they are stereotyped and often on an elementary level, needing little or no demonstration or discovery

44. Whenever possible, a filmstrip should be used rather than a sound motion picture on the same subject because
    1. it takes less time to show it
    2. it is usually more sequential
    3. it can be used to focus attention more readily where the teacher desires it
    4. the absence of a sound-track removes a distraction
    5. it is usually better prepared since it deals directly with the topic

45. In order to complete the course of study with a class of slow learners, the teacher should
    1. skip certain sections which are too difficult
    2. have pupils take copious notes from the blackboard to be studied at home
    3. have pupils read the textbook in class under his direction
    4. plan for varied methods of study of the essential concepts of each unit
    5. make a précis of the remaining work and distribute it in mimeographed form to the students

46. Of the following possible questions for various science lessons, the one which BEST meets the criteria for a good teaching question is
    1. Isn't it a fact that the stamen contains the anther?
    2. What about the piston?
    3. What is diastrophism and what theory is used to explain it?
    4. What is the word that denotes a central part or thing about which other parts of things are grouped? It is a six-letter word that begins with n and ends with s.
    5. Why do glaciers reach beyond the snow line?

47. The MOST important value of a lesson plan book is to
    1. insure continuity of instruction in the event of the teacher's absence
    2. permit the supervisor to evaluate the quality of work done
    3. enable the teacher to give thought to the work that will be carried on in the class
    4. enable the teacher to dictate important statements
    5. assure that there will be no repetition of work previously covered

48. Reinforcing learning can BEST be achieved when drill is
    1. given to all pupils regardless of achievement
    2. given in intensive doses
    3. individualized
    4. given without motivation
    5. consistent, continuous, and culminating

49. Thought provoking answers are MOST easily achieved when
    1. a pupil's name is called before a question is asked
    2. a question is repeated several times in varied forms
    3. a question is asked and then a pupil is called upon to recite
    4. pupils anticipate the question
    5. pupils are advised to think before they speak

50. The teaching effectiveness of class discussions can be improved by all of the following EXCEPT having
    1. pupils face one another in speaking
    2. a competent recorder write main contributions on the blackboard
    3. the brighter pupils offer most of the contributions
    4. the group evaluate its own performance in terms of previously accepted objectives
    5. pupils ask questions of each other and of the teacher

KEY (CORRECT ANSWERS)

1.	2	11.	1	21.	1	31.	4	41.	1
2.	1	12.	3	22.	2	32.	1	42.	1
3.	3	13.	3	23.	3	33.	4	43.	2
4.	5	14.	2	24.	3	34.	1	44.	3
5.	2	15.	2	25.	5	35.	3	45.	4
6.	3	16.	2	26.	1	36.	4	46.	5
7.	3	17.	1	27.	3	37.	5	47.	3
8.	5	18.	3	28.	3	38.	1	48.	3
9.	2	19.	1	29.	2	39.	1	49.	3
10.	4	20.	3	30.	5	40.	2	50.	3

TEST 2

DIRECTIONS: Each question or incomplete statement is followed by several suggested answers or completions. Select the one that BEST answers the question or completes the statement.

1. A slow learner should be expected to do all of the following EXCEPT to
   1. do brief written assignments
   2. work as hard as other pupils
   3. spend much of the day in manual art and fine art classes
   4. master a modified curriculum
   5. answer questions orally or in writing after watching a television program at home

2. In a class where the majority of pupils have I.Q.'s lower than 85, GREATEST emphasis should be placed on which one of the following?
   1. game-like activities for sensory-motor training
   2. committee reports based on group research
   3. drill and review activities
   4. copying diagrams and charts from the textbook
   5. adaptation of subject matter to the interests and needs of the pupils

3. In a class where the majority of pupils are retarded in reading, the predominating activity should be
   1. written work of one kind or another
   2. film and filmstrip lessons
   3. developmental lessons of various types
   4. phonics lessons based on the textbook
   5. supervised study followed by short quizzes of the objective type

4. In a science class, the children's first-hand, out-of-school experiences should
   1. form the basis of the entire science course
   2. be supplemented and reinforced by the course of study
   3. constitute at least 50% of the science course
   4. be ignored if they have little direct relation to the course of study
   5. be built upon to structure the course of study

5. Of the following statements, select the one which is NOT consistent with present thinking.
   1. All pupils can be expected to discover mathematical relationships completely on their own initiative.
   2. Drilling pupils on the solution of problems of the same type offers them limited experience in problem solving.
   3. In general, success in problem-solving depends, in part, upon finding a relationship between the known and the unknown.
   4. Not every textbook exercise is a problem.
   5. Computational items should be included with problem-solving items in drawing up a unit test.

6. Of the following statements concerning methods of teaching, the one which is NOT correct is:
   1. In the lecture method, there may well be a great deal of teaching but little learning.
   2. In the laboratory method, students weigh, count, draw, measure, compare and analyze.
   3. Teachers who tend to move on rapidly, may not provide sufficient time for experimentation and for self-discovery.
   4. An important method in the development of concepts is the use of a work book.
   5. Supervised study as a method of teaching may be used to great advantage with certain groups or in certain situations.

7. Of the following, which one is the MOST acceptable procedure for spurring pupils to greater effort in their work?
   1. Have each pupil keep a graph of his test marks
   2. Read all test scores aloud in class
   3. Give pupils test marks without returning test papers to them
   4. Return test papers to pupils without informing them of the test grades
   5. Keep pupils guessing and uncertain about their test marks so that the possibility of "coasting" by those who score high is eliminated

8. Which one of the following is the MOST effective way of allowing for individual rates of progress in class work?
   1. Omit difficult and time-consuming topics
   2. Teach all topics with variations of depth and intensity
   3. Concentrate on review of fundamentals
   4. Have slow learners work principally with work book assignments to give them greater drill opportunities
   5. Always assign extra-credit homework problems or test items

9. In planning drill for classes, which one of the following procedures should be adhered to?
   1. Every pupil in a class should be assigned the same drill exercises
   2. An entire lesson period should frequently be devoted to drill exercises
   3. Drill should be individualized according to pupil need
   4. The teacher should consistently use the same drill technique
   5. Drill should occupy 40-50% of each lesson

10. Which one of the following is the LEAST effective way of enriching mathematics courses for bright pupils?
    1. Assembling bibliographies of mathematics and science books in the school library and encouraging wide reading
    2. Publishing a mathematics departmental magazine each year
    3. Arranging a mathematics section in the school's annual Science Fair
    4. Holding a mathematics test contest
    5. Making sure that the bright pupils complete all of the more difficult exercises and problems of each set in the assigned text

11. The BEST homework assignment to assist junior high school pupils to prepare for a test is which one of the following?
    1. To tell them to study for a test
    2. To give them a set of problems identical to those that will appear on the test
    3. To tell them to prepare a set of questions they think should appear on the test
    4. To tell them the scope of the test and to assign specific study references and specific practice material covering the scope
    5. To tell them to re-read and study certain chapters in the textbook

12. Which one of the following statements is CONTRARY to present thinking?
    1. Most teachers regard homework as important.
    2. Experimental evidence is not clearly convincing that homework is truly important.
    3. The voluntary type of assignment in which the pupil does whatever he thinks is necessary is the solution to the homework dilemma.
    4. Many parents think homework is helpful.
    5. Homework should take a variety of forms in addition to the written assignment.

13. Which of the following is the BEST approach to the use of the text book by a teacher?
    1. Only as a source of practice exercises
    2. Primarily as a source of problems to be placed on tests
    3. To assist pupils in learning how to read explanations of new concepts and techniques
    4. Primarily for review
    5. Primarily as the course of study to be mastered

14. Of the following, the LEAST proper use of the textbook is as
    1. a quick view of things to be learned
    2. a minimum for which pupils may be held responsible
    3. the course of study
    4. a reference for pictures, maps, graphs, tables
    5. a source for homework assignments

15. Of the following statements concerning questioning, which one is NOT consistent with current thinking?
    1. Some questions, though perfect in form, may challenge only a limited number of pupils.
    2. Vague and incomplete questions tend to confuse pupils.
    3. "Chorus" answers do not afford all pupils an opportunity to think.
    4. The skillful teacher is a skillful questioner.
    5. Questions starting with "why" and "how" should generally be avoided.

16. Of the following, select the suggestion LEAST likely to help a pupil having difficulty in finding the solution to a verbal problem
    1. Generalize the problem by using letters instead of numbers
    2. Estimate the answer
    3. Use round numbers
    4. Use diagrams or representations
    5. Refer to real situations

17. Of the following, the statement which is NOT descriptive of a characteristic of a good drill is that
    1. the exercises are graded
    2. understanding precedes the drill
    3. complex processes are emphasized
    4. the drill is addressed to pupil weaknesses
    5. drills are given when needed

18. Tests should be given
    1. daily   2. at the completion of a unit
    3. without previous notice   4. weekly
    5. to check upon the homework assignment

19. Standardized group tests are used more frequently than individual tests   because
    1. the same amount of time is needed to test a whole class by a grouped approach as a single pupil by an individual approach
    2. group tests give better results than individual tests
    3. group tests have primary, intermediate and advanced forms whereas individual tests have only one form
    4. no training is needed to administer a group test
    5. they are more economical to administer

20. Of the following statements about marks, the one which is NOT correct is
    1. Excessive emphasis on marks may cause the pupil to consider the mark more important than the material to be learned.
    2. The pupil may rely too heavily on mere memory in order to get high marks.
    3. Occasionally, overemphasis on marks may lead to cheating.
    4. Marks based solely on written tests give a valid measure of a pupil's achievement, because they are always objective.
    5. Marks are an important index of a pupil's ability .

21. Standardized achievement tests are characterized by all of the following principles EXCEPT
    1. They often show differing results, depending upon the particular form of the test used
    2. They are administered in accordance with uniform procedures indicated in the manual of instructions
    3. They have norms for grade or age
    4. They are scored in accordance with standard procedures indicated in the manual of insttuctions
    5. They are helpful in evaluating the achievement of a class, a school, a district, a city

22. Of the following, the PRIME purpose of grouping pupils is to
    1. develop social attitudes
    2. separate unrule pupils
    3. provide the teacher with a smaller range of pupil ability or disability
    4. help solve book shortages
    5. encourage individual achievement

23. Of these statements concerning grouping, select the one which is CONTRARY to present day thinking:
    1. Grouping enables the teacher to meet individual differences.
    2. Results of inventory tests may be used as one of the bases for forming groups.

3. Teachers should avoid attaching any status value to groups.
4. Once in a group, a pupil should be kept there for the rest of the year.
5. Training in committee duties and responsibilities are valuable outcomes of grouping.

24. Of the following statements about slow pupils, the one which is MOST NEARLY correct is that they
    1. are always unruly
    2. should be given plenty of busy work
    3. usually have a short attention span
    4. should seldom be given homework
    5. should be closely supervised and given intensive instructions and directions at all times

25. Of these statements concerning the use of the overhead projector, which one is NOT true?
    1. It may not be used with a page of the textbook.
    2. It enables the teacher to observe the class reaction.
    3. It may be used with transparencies and with overlays.
    4. It requires an additional person to operate it.
    5. It does not require involved handling or intricate instructions and directions.

26. Of these statements concerning the use of audio-visual aids, which one is NOT true?
    1. Students are helped to learn faster.
    2. They help students to gain more accurate information.
    3. They help students to perceive and understand meanings.
    4. They serve to concretize verbalisms.
    5. They substitute for, rather than supplement, instructional techniques.

27. Homework should be assigned regularly in the junior high school, because, among other values,
    1. doing homework aids in the development of more independent study habits
    2. survey results indicate that pupil progress is proportional to the amount of homework assigned
    3. homework keeps pupils out of mischief at home
    4. it is traditional to assign homework, and parents demand it
    5. homework supplements or supplies what the teacher did not teach in the lesson

28. In planning a homework assignment, the teacher should observe which one of the following principles?
    1. The assignment should review material previously taught as well as material taught on the day that the assignment was given
    2. The assignment should be limited to material taught on the day that the assignment was given
    3. The assignment should not include any material taught on the day the assignment was given
    4. The assignment should be done only by those pupils who have not fallen so far behind that they cannot profit from doing the assignment
    5. The assignment should include some form of written work each day

29. All of the following are desirable educational practices EXCEPT
    1. starting the lesson promptly at the beginning of the period
    2. completing the lesson even if the class has to be detained a few minutes
    3. planning a motivation for each lesson
    4. eliciting the lesson aim from the pupils
    5. basing the lesson on some controversial current topic

30. All of the following items apply to the use of classroom demonstrations EXCEPT that the
    1. apparatus used should be as complex as possible
    2. demonstration should be visible to everyone in the room
    3. demonstration should be tried out in advance
    4. purpose of the demonstration should be clear
    5. demonstration should serve as a springboard for the lesson

31. All of the following are good techniques in handling a homework assignment EXCEPT that it should be
    1. given automatically and without explanation
    2. an outgrowth of the lesson
    3. a mixture of thought and fact problems
    4. of reasonable length and difficulty
    5. of varying form, e.g., a written assignment, a reading assignment, a research assignment

32. A test which measures that which it sets out to measure is said to be which one of the following?
    1. consistent   2. subjective   3. valid   4. reliable
    5. objective

33. Of the following, a technique that is especially useful for the study of inter-pupil relationships in a group or classroom situation is the
    1. anecdotal record   2. sociogram
    3. Rorschach Test   4. Thematic Apperception Test
    5. group interview

34. A temporary psychological adjustment wherein one attributes one's faults, weaknesses, and wishes to others is called
    1. regression   2. projection   3. repression   4. sublimation
    5. rationalization

35. If a pupil mispronounces a word, the teacher should
    1. ignore the error
    2. interrupt the recitation to correct the mispronunciation
    3. incidentally correct the error in an unobtrusive fashion
    4. give the pupil a lower mark
    5. prepare a special lesson for one full period on words commonly mispronounced

36. All of the following are objections to the use of punishment EXCEPT
    1. The results of punishment are less predictable than the results of reward.
    2. Punishment occasionally fixes the punished behavior rather than eliminates it.
    3. The danger of injustice in punishment because of unintended and disproportionate emotional upset is real.

4. Punishment is often inconsonant with the aims of society and the educational philosophy of the school.
5. Prompt punishment sometimes reduces anxiety by clarifying the limits for allowable behavior.

37. The book SLUMS AND SUBURBS was written by
   1. James Conant
   2. Richard Hofstadter
   3. Harold Howe II
   4. Theodore H. White
   5. Martin Mayer

38. A pupil has been transferred from one class to another. The previous teacher informs the new teacher that the student is uncooperative and does not work up to his academic potential. With respect to the information received, which of the following procedures is the one the new teacher should attempt FIRST?
   1. Use highly structured lessons as a means of gaining student cooperation
   2. Reserve judgement until a number of lessons have been taught
   3. Discuss the situation with her supervisor
   4. Make a special effort to organize highly motivated lessons
   5. Visit the pupil's home and interview the parents

39. A child openly defies the teacher. He runs to his seat where he mutters to himself. The teacher should
   1. go to the child's desk quickly to find out what he is saying
   2. ask his best friend to calm him down
   3. immediately send a note to her supervisor asking her to come to the room
   4. use the "section manager's technique" -order him to shut up- or else
   5. set up a situation in which he need not take part and proceed with the lesson

40. A pupil in a high school accuses a classmate of stealing a quarter from his desk. The teacher should
   1. suggest that the two pupils settle the matter after school hours
   2. stop whatever she is doing and try to determine the truth of the matter
   3. suggest to both pupils that they remain after class to talk with her
   4. send the two pupils to the principal's office
   5. incisively tell them to grow up and act like mature young people, pointing out how ridiculous it is to fight over so small an amount as twenty-five cents

41. The teacher will BEST promote learning by
   1. pointing out the errors of her pupils
   2. finding something in every child's contribution to praise
   3. making appropriate corrections of pupils' work
   4. having pupils repeat work until corrections are unnecessary
   5. promptly marking and returning all written work, with corrections clearly indicated

42. A teacher plans to write some anecdotal observations of children in her class. Of the following, the *BEST* example of the type of anecdotal comment to be written is:
    1. "Irresponsible at times. I believe there is not enough supervision in Jack's house."
    2. "Joan bought candy for the children again. She is a darling"
    3. "When my back was turned, spitballs were thrown. Fred is at it again."
    4. "The stapler is missing. What a thief Manuel has turned out to be!"
    5. "Stewart did not participate in the basketball game again today. He sat and watched."

43. Of the following, the *MOST* important consideration for the teacher in planning her work is
    1. fostering the development of good interpersonal relationships among her pupils
    2. insuring good scholastic achievement on the part of her pupils
    3. adapting her instruction to the limitations of her pupils' abilities
    4. fostering the development of good integration of her pupils and those in the other grades
    5. to see that the course of study is completely covered

44. Of the following, the *MOST* important purpose in teacher planning is to
    1. provide a permanent record and schedule of topics to be taught
    2. make certain that all curricular areas are included
    3. make sure that the teacher gives adequate thought to the instructional program
    4. insure the proper organization and functioning of groups
    5. ensure the safety, happiness, and welfare of all the children

45. The teacher should plan her program for the day with the pupils. It is *MOST* important that this plan should be
    1. followed without deviation, since the pupils need a structured situation
    2. entered in the teacher's plan book at the close of the day
    3. used as a tentative guide, to be changed at the teacher's discretion
    4. checked and evaluated at the end of the day
    5. so structured as to call for at least one recitation from each pupil in the class

46. A teacher of a primary class notices that many children who formerly put on their outer clothing without help have begun to ask for asistance. The teacher should
    1. refuse to help with their clothing
    2. report the matter to their parents
    3. have them stay after class and show them that they can do it
    4. have them assist the children who really need the help
    5. have them reassigned to a slow class

47. In developing modeling experiences with pupils, teachers should use ceramic clay rather than plasticine because the former
    1. is more sanitary
    2. is less expensive
    3. is easier to store
    4. is more readily available
    5. gives better tactile satisfaction

48. The teacher of a primary class wishes to initiate an art project involving brush painting. The *BEST* media to use would be a
    1. camel's hair brush and tempera paint
    2. wide brush and tempera paint
    3. wide brush and oil paint
    4. narrow brush and oil paint
    5. camel's hair brush and oil paint

49. One of the boys in a class insists on wearing a sweater in class in spite of the teacher's request to remove it. She should
    1. ignore it so as to avoid embarrassment
    2. send for a parent immediately
    3. explain to the boy how and why her request is related to his health
    4. refer the case to the principal
    5. order him to take it off

50. A girl in a class has been repeatedly taking things that do not belong to her. The teacher should
    1. seat the girl by herself, away from the rest of the class, so as to avoid temptation
    2. call for the parent to discuss this and get her cooperation
    3. discuss the topic of stealing with the class without mentioning the girl's name
    4. ask the girl to return the things she has taken and explain why it was wrong for her to have taken them
    5. send the girl to the clinic for a free psychiatric examination

KEY (CORRECT ANSWERS)

1.	3	11.	4	21.	1	31.	1	41.	2
2.	5	12.	3	22.	3	32.	3	42.	5
3.	3	13.	3	23.	4	33.	2	43.	3
4.	2	14.	3	24.	3	34.	2	44.	3
5.	1	15.	5	25.	4	35.	3	45.	4
6.	4	16.	1	26.	5	36.	5	46.	4
7.	1	17.	3	27.	1	37.	1	47.	5
8.	2	18.	2	28.	1	38.	2	48.	2
9.	3	19.	1	29.	2	39.	5	49.	3
10.	5	20.	4	30.	1	40.	3	50.	2

BASIC PRINCIPLES AND PRACTICES IN EDUCATION
THE NEW PROGRAM OF EDUCATION

I. PHILOSOPHY AND OBJECTIVES

A. PHILOSOPHY
  1. An analysis of the aims and purposes of education
  2. An appraisal of current educational practices
  3. A statement of the "ideal" to be attained
  4. A justification of the means to be employed
B. CONCEPTS OF EDUCATION
  1. Education as knowledge
     a. Emphasis on factual learning
     b. Transmitting the past heritage
     c. Excessive use of texts
  2. Education as discipline
     a. Training the memory, imagination, etc.
     b. Emphasis on rote memory, drill, frequent tests, etc.
     c. Reliance on theory of transfer of training
  3. Education as growth
     a. Developing latent capacities and realization of child's potentialities
     b. Experiential and functional learning
     c. Emphasis on attitudes, appreciations, and interests
     d. Child-centered curriculum
     e. Stress on social relationships and democratic living procedures
C. OBJECTIVES
  1. Character - ethical living in a society promoting the common welfare
  2. American Heritage - faith in American democracy and respect for dignity and worth of the individual regardless of race, religion, nationality or socio-economic status
  3. Health - sound body and wholesome mental and emotional development
  4. Exploration - discovery and development of individual aptitudes
  5. Thinking - develop ability to reason critically, using facts and principles
  6. Knowledges and skills - command of common integrating knowledges and skills
  7. Appreciation and expression - appreciation and enjoyment of beauty and development of powers of creative expression
  8. Social relationships - develop desirable social relationships at home, in school, in the community
  9. Economic relationships - appreciation of economic processes and of contributions of all who serve in the world of work

  MNEMONIC DEVICE FOR REMEMBERING THESE OBJECTIVES

  T hinking   K nowledges and skills
  E xploration   A ppreciation
  A merican heritage   S ocial relationships
  C haracter   E conomic relationships
  H ealth

D. METHOD OF ACHIEVING THESE OBJECTIVES
  1. Former emphasis on content with limited worthwhile, real experiences. Present stress on experiences with content used as a means to an end rather than as an end in itself.
  2. This calls for a reorganization of our courses of study. Organization will now be in related areas rather than in separate isolated syllabi.
  These areas include:
     a. Pupil participation - to include planning, routines, and housekeeping, responsibilities, exploring school and community activities.
     b. Health - to include health instruction and guidance, safety education, rest, recreation, emotional adjustment, nutrition.
     c. Art - to include experimenting, use of various media as means of expression, practical applications in home, school, and community.
     d. Music - vocal, instrumental, rhythmic for enjoyment, expression, and understanding.
     e. Language Arts - reading, literature, composition, spelling, penmanship, speech, listening, dramatization.
     f. Social Studies - history, geography, civics, character, family relationships, consumer problems, intercultural education, citizenship and concepts of democracy.
     g. Science - nature study, weather, plants and soil, animals, earth and sky, food and water, tools and instruments, simple machines and electrical devices, flightcraft.
     h. Arithmetic - size, space, distance, time, weight, concepts, computations, problem solving.

MNEMONIC DEVICE FOR THESE AREAS
H ealth   L anguage Arts
A rithmetic   A rt
S ocial Studies   M usic
                    P upil participation
                    S cience

E. ORGANISMIC PSYCHOLOGY *(our current program is based chiefly on these principles)*
  1. The principle of continuous growth - This emphasizes the flexible, experimental, emergent nature of the individual and of society; it stresses the continuity of experience. (Aspects: continuous progress plan; constant curriculum revision.)
  2. The principle of experience as the method of learning - This emphasizes learning through functional, real experiences as opposed to memorization, drill, dictated assignments, etc. (Aspects: excursions; planning; research; reporting.)
  3. The principal of integration - This emphasizes the wholeness and unity of individuals and of society. It stresses the interaction between the learner and the learning situation and demands maximum life-likeness in learning situations. (Aspects: units; use of community resources; large areas of instruction; larger time-block

F. UNDERLYING TENETS OF THE PROGRAM
  1. Education of the whole child - social, civic, intellectual, ethica vocational
  2. Learning through real, functional experiences (activity vs. passivity)

3. The "intangibles" as an important end of education (interests, attitudes, character, etc.)
4. The concept of the child-centered school as opposed to the subject-centered school
5. The inclusion of the nine objectives of education as a part of educational planning at every step

G. WHAT DOES THE NEW PROGRAM MEAN?
1. These things are basic:
   a. Socialization of procedures
   b. Integration of personality (before integration of subject matter)
   c. Increased pupil-teacher participation in planning and evaluating the educative process
   d. Group procedures
   e. A program to meet the individual's time-table of growth as well as a general development time-table
   f. First-hand experiencing as a "must" in education
   g. A mental hygiene viewpoint for the teacher
   h. Closer relationship between school-life and life in the world outside
   i. An acceptance of the view that concomitant learnings can sometimes be more important than the original learnings to be taught
2. It is NOT merely:
   a. Unit development
   b. Correlation of subject matter
   c. Working through committees
   d. Provision for research activities
   e. Emphasis on reporting and discussion
   f. Planning for a culmination
   g. Keeping diaries and logs

H. ADVANTAGES AND DISADVANTAGES
1. Proponents of the New Program maintain that this program:
   a. Provides a flexible content
   b. Encourages individual aptitudes
   c. Permits much practice in social behavior
   d. Encourages independent learning
   e. Encourages creative expression
   f. Provides a vitalized curriculum
   g. Permits greater integration of subject matter
   h. Provides for leisure-time activities
   i. Provides a success program for each child
   j. Makes greater provision for diagnosis, guidance, and individual remedial treatment
   k. Contributes abundantly towards the development of good character
2. Opponents of the New Program maintain that:
   a. There is no gradation of the difficulties of different units of work
   b. It is not true to life (since life is not a series of activities)
   c. Too much reliance is placed on incidental learning
   d. There is no provision for participation by every child
   e. Teachers have not been trained sufficiently
   f. Equipment is underemphasized
   g. The interests of children are not sufficient as a guide for subject matter

      h. The superficial aspects are overemphasized
      i. Many important "learnings" are omitted
      j. No provision is made for duplication in the case of pupils who are transferred or admitted
I. TRADITIONAL VS. PROGRESSIVE EDUCATION

TRADITIONAL   *PROGRESSIVE*

1. PHILOSOPHY

TRADITIONAL	PROGRESSIVE
a. School is a preparation for life	a. School is "life itself"
b. Emphasis on social heritage	b. Development of whole personality-knowledge, attitudes, morals, health
c. Adjust pipil to society that arises	c. School aims to improve society

2. CURRICULUM

TRADITIONAL	PROGRESSIVE
a. Factual curriculum laid out in advance for all	a. Subject matter - vital, purposeful, integrated, flexible, follows child's interests
b. Subjects clearly separated and isolated	b. Long units, integration and correlation of subject matter
c. Emphasis on memorization	c. Learning through experiences
d. Slavish use of text books	d. Use of a variety of reference and source materials

3. ROLE OF TEACHER

TRADITIONAL	PROGRESSIVE
a. Dominant factor in the learning process	a. Teacher is a guide and helper
b. Pupil passivity	b. Socialization and maximum pupil participation

4. METHODS

TRADITIONAL	PROGRESSIVE
a. Stressed mastery of subject matter	a. Adjustment of curriculum to needs, interests, and capacities of each child
b. Isolated drills. Extrinsic	b. Functional learning. Individualized drill at the point of error. Intrinsic
c. Rigid, formal discipline	c. A hum of activity. Self-discipline. Social adjustment
d. Inside of schoolroom	d. Excursions and field trips

5. SUPERVISION

TRADITIONAL	PROGRESSIVE
a. Dictatorial and inflexible	a. Democratic, scientific, creative
b. Teachers rated according to ability in achieving grade standards (standardized tests)	b. Teachers judged on basis of their ability to promote desirable attitudes - interests, appreciations, etc. (attitude test and case histories)

J. GENERAL PRINCIPLES IN ANY MODERN PHILOSOPHY OF ELEMENTARY EDUCATION
  1. Education must be democratic, universal, and compulsory
  2. There must be a unifying philosophy for the school system as a whole
  3. This philosophy must be essentially a social philosophy; the school must adjust children to a changing social order
  4. The curriculum must be flexible and must be subject to frequent (continuous) revision
  5. There must be flexibility in classroom procedures
  6. Adequate equipment must be provided
  7. Adequate provision must be made for the mentally and physically handicapped

II. THE CURRICULUM

A. DEFINITIONS
  1. The *CURRICULUM* consists of all the experiences, including all the subject matter and skills, which are utilized and interpreted by the school to further the aims of education. These experiences result from interaction between persons, influences, and material facilities. Some of the factors which effect the curriculum are:
     a. The political, economic, and social structure of the surrounding society
     b. The public opinion toward education
     c. The aims and philosophies of those operating the educational system
     d. The decisions concerning methods and materials, teacher selection, sarlaries, and physical plant
     e. The course of study, or, more properly, the documents made available to the teachers
  2. Early *COURSES OF STUDY* usually consisted only of a subject-matter outline; later ones included also some suggested learning activities, teaching procedures, diagnostic devices, and evaluation techniques. The emphasis, in all instances, was on "prescribed" subject matter to be covered, and some courses of study even specified the number of minutes per day to be devoted to each of the segments and the specific fact questions to be used.
  3. Modern *GUIDES* for teachers are not usually called courses of study. They suggest a wealth of materials and experiences; far from minimizing subject matter, they suggest more of it better adapted for use with varying levels of abilities and interests. They include bulletins on:
     a. the teaching of various subjects
     b. the organization of experience units with subject lines disregarded
     c. the characteristics of children
     d. varied learning experiences
     e. teaching procedures
     f. ways of using different types and amounts of subject matter
     g. sources of instructional aids
     h. evaluational techniques
     i. bibliographies, etc.

B. GENERAL CONSIDERATIONS
  1. A curriculum develops in answer to the needs of a group of learners and to the demands of a given society.
  2. A curriculum is made by a teacher and her pupils as they work together in the school.
  3. The development of a specific curriculum is a cooperative activity in which many persons participate (superintendents, principals, teachers, subject-matter specialists, consultants, school psychologists, pupils, parents, social agencies, advisory commissions, etc.)
  4. A program of curriculum improvement involves a study of:
     a. the political, economic, and social structure of the surrounding society
     b. public opinion toward education
     c. advice or information for the public
     d. the aims and philosophy of current educational practice

   e. the abilities, needs, purposes and individual differences among the learners
   f. the origin and nature of subject matter
   g. the development of present curriculums
   h. the nature of modern outcomes of learning
   i. the many new techniques of evaluation
  5. A program of curriculum improvement is far broader than the writing of a course of study or series of teachers' guides; it is concerned with the improvement of living and learning conditions in the school and in the community of which it is a part.
  6. A program of curriculum improvement should result in changes of attitudes, appreciations, and skills on the part of the participants and in important changes in the learning situation.
C. CONDITIONS THAT COMPEL CURRICULAR CHANGES
  1. Technological developments - In a society where most people work for someone else, it is important that the curriculum emphasize the attitudes and skills of cooperation.
  2. International problems - The curriculum must emphasize international understanding as well as the defense of America and other freedom-loving nations.
  3. Social change - The curriculum must prepare children for living in a complex and changing world, and must emphasize moral responsibility for one's acts both as an individual as well as a member of a group.
  4. Educational progress - The increase of available materials of instruction and the expanding role of the teacher call for a redistribution of teachers' time and energies in terms of a new set of values.
D. CHANGES THAT RESULT FROM CURRICULUM IMPROVEMENT
  1. In the professional staff-cooperative planning; working together on educational problems; experimentation with promising procedures; study of human growth and development.
  2. In the teaching-learning situation - improvement in the school plant, equipment, and supplies; use of community resources; available community services; opportunities for children to participate in community life.
  3. In improved pupil behavior - ability to define and solve meaningful problems: development of new interest; self-evaluation; skill in communication; skill in human relations; initiative; creativeness.
  4. In community relationships - participation by lay citizens; public support; public relations.
  5. In school organization - plan of organization; staff selection procedures; school size; class size; daily schedules; district services; faculty conferences.
  6. In instructional materials - cooperative production of instructional materials; more effective use of commercial materials; better selection of teaching aids; establishment of a "materials center"; development of a professional library.
  7. In ways of working together - teacher-pupil planning; group dynamics; sociometric techniques; intergroup education.
E. MAIN PROBLEMS IN CURRICULUM DEVELOPMENT
  1. The determination of educational directions
  2. The selection of experiences comprising the educational program
  3. The selection of a pattern of curriculum organization

4. The determination of principles and procedures by which the curriculum can be evaluated and changed
F. FACTORS AFFECTING CURRICULUM DEVELOPMENT
  1. The existing political, economic, and social structure
  2. Pressure exerted by minority groups or vested interests
  3. Legislation
  4. Tradition
  5. Influence of logically organized subject matter and compartmentalization
  6. Textbooks
G. CONSIDERATIONS FOR CURRICULUM PROGRAMS
  1. The improvement program is to be developed with the aid of supervisors, teachers, pupils, parents, and community.
  2. The curriculum should be readily adaptable to individual differences, needs, and interests and to the special needs of groups, schools and communities.
  3. There should be provision for articulation between and among the various divisions and levels of the school system.
  4. There must be provision for continuous experimentation and research.
  5. There must be flexibility and allowance for interpretation and change to meet new situations and conditions.
  6. There must be provision for evaluation of principles, practices, and outcomes, as well as for appraisal of the curriculum improvement program itself.
  7. The curriculum must provide conditions, situations, and activities favorable to the continuous growth and progress of each individual.
  8. Curriculum policies and practices should encourage friendly understanding and democratic relations among supervisors, teachers, pupils and parents.
  9. The success of a curriculum is dependent on competent leadership. (Supervision interprets and implements the curriculum and seeks to improve teaching and learning; teachers' attitudes and understandings determine the effectiveness of the curriculum; community aims, purposes, and resources exert an important influence on the curriculum; pupils help in developing a wholesome pattern of democratic living in which the curriculum operates most effectively.)
H. QUESTIONS RELATED TO CURRICULUM DEVELOPMENT
  1. Why is the traditional curriculum, used with seeming success for years, now under such criticism, analysis, and change?
  2. Is the curriculum an instrument of social progress?
  3. Should the aims of education and the content of the curriculum be determined with some definiteness in advance of actual teaching-learning situations?
  4. Is all, none, or a given part of the curriculum to be required of all learners - regardless of origin, present status, and very probable destiny?
  5. How shall the curriculum be organized - scope and sequence determined?
  6. How shall the curriculum content be selected?
  7. What are the desired outcomes of learning experiences?
  8. How much of the curriculum can be formulated by the pupils?
  9. What stand shall the curriculum take on "indoctrination?"

10. What procedures should be used in reconstructing the curriculum?
11. What are the criteria for evaluating a curriculum?

III. GROUPING AND COMMITTEE WORK

A. ORGANIZING GROUPS FOR INSTRUCTION
   1. Know the children before you group
      a. General level of achievement (standardized tests)
      b. Individual problems in the area (everyday performance)
      c. Capacity to achieve (expectancy)
      d. Personal and social adjustment (sociogram)
   2. Develop a "readiness" for grouping
      a. Teach the techniques that will be the basis for independent activity later
      b. Be familiar with the types of exercises to be used for group work later; anticipate some of the skills which will be required
      c. Develop work-skills (choosing something, sharing materials, working independently, etc.)
   3. Launch the best group first
      a. The first group will be those children most advanced intellectually and socially
      b. The remainder of the class learns to work independently as the teacher works with the first group
      c. As both these groups learn to work simultaneously, the teacher notes the point at which further subdivision becomes necessary (for example, the slower group may be broken down into a normal and slow group)
   4. Group standards should be set cooperatively by the teacher and class
   5. Some abilities to aim for:
      a. Working alone
      b. Working quietly
      c. Completing a job
      d. Moving to the next job when the present one is completed
      e. Finding and correcting one's errors
      f. Evaluating one's own work
   6. Arrangement of pupils
      a. Reduce to a minimum the interference of one group with another (through location of groups in the room, allocation of blackboard space, etc.)
      b. Have a group's materials placed near to where that group works
B. CRITERIA FOR GROUP WORK
   1. Are the procedures used in accordance with the techniques advocated in the program of education?
      a. What is the basis on which the groups are set up? (Common weaknesses, sociogram, etc.)
      b. Is the goal for each group set and understood?
      c. Have these goals been set by cooperative planning?
      d. In what type of activity is the group engaged - individual or group? Is there a free interplay of minds at all times?
      e. Are there evidences of evaluation within the group - by individuals and by the group?
      f. What is the extent and variety of materials used?
   2. Are there evidences of individual contributions by children in the group?

3. Are there evidences of committee work of children (charts, etc.)?
  4. Are there evidences of teacher-supervision of group procedures?
  5. Are there evidences of the growth of social skills, attitudes, and understandings of social living?
C. COMMITTEE WORK
  1. Group dynamics as a factor in committee work
     a. Sociograms and friendship charts
     b. Place of the "stars"
     c. Working the isolates into the committee
  2. As in grouping, the teacher starts with a single-committee and develops committee techniques with the members
  3. Selection of a chairman and a secretary by the committee - importance of leadership and followership
  4. Contributions of the members of a committee toward the solution of a problem - working together and all that it implies
  5. Place of the teacher
     a. She never "abdicates her position;" she advises and guides when indicated
     b. She watches closely those members with personal problems
     c. She anticipates difficulties in human relations
     d. She assigns a place for the committee to work comfortably
     e. She displays charts listing the committees, with leaders starred
     f. She makes available materials for research, including pictorial material and special materials for the non-reader or retarded reader
     g. She checks the progress of the group and of the individuals in the group regularly (before a reporting period, etc.)
  6. Standards for group work periods
     NOTE: These are suggestions for charts
     a. For a Group Leader
        a.1 Know what work to do each day
        a.2 Keep the group working
        a.3 Do not be too bossy
     b. For the Group
        b.1 We will speak softly
        b.2 We will talk only to our own group
        b.3 We will talk only about our own work
        b.4 We will try to find our own materials
        b.5 We will use our time wisely
        b.6 We will clean up when we have finished
     c. For Groups preparing a report
        c.1 Skim books for stories on the topic of your report
        c.2 Plan an outline of the whole topic
        c.3 Choose sub-topics for study
        c.4 Work on topics - make an outline, do some research, make something, etc.
        c.5 Give your report to the group for criticism
        c.6 Give the report to the class

IV. EVALUATION

A. ITEMS TO BE EVALUATED
  1. Mental development *(traditionally, this has been almost the sole emphasis)*
  2. Physical aspects

       3. Social aspects
       4. Emotional aspects
B. REASONS FOR EVALUATING
    1. It is a means of discovering group and individual growth
    2. It is a means of discovering whether children are developing at a rate commensurate with their general capacity (expectancy)
    3. To discover children's strengths and weaknesses, and necessity for specific help (diagnostic) in particular cases
    4. To indicate to the school how it can best provide the conditions of growth that make learning most economical and most effective
    5. Children learn more effectively when they take part in evaluation
       a. As members of a group, they learn to become aware of group needs (through learning they must acquire for a specific purpose)
       b. They learn how to plan for group needs (through practice in evaluating possible courses of action)
       c. They learn to take stock as they proceed with their tasks (through evaluating progress periodically)
       d. They learn ways of deciding when their project has reached a satisfactory conclusion (through practice in evaluating their achievements in the light of their original objectives)
C. WHEN TO EVALUATE
    1. It is a continuing activity, taking place at every stage of the learning process *(Evaluation is not concerned solely with end products)*
    2. The teacher evaluates situations as they occur
    3. "The quality of living" that goes on in a classroom is evaluated as an indication of class morale
    4. The amount of communication that takes place is, at all times, a significant evaluative factor
    5. The need for recording social adjustments, emotional maturity, attention span, language development, interests, and enthusiasms of children makes continuous evaluation a necessity
    6. Check lists and anecdotal records may be used to record what is observed
D. WHO EVALUATES?
    1. Everyone concerned in the educative process should take part in evaluation
       a. The children, with or without the guidance of the teacher, make valid judgments
       b. The teacher evaluates herself, the effectiveness of her procedures, the progress of her class and the individuals therein, the climate of her room, and the classroom situation
       c. The school, as a composite of teachers and supervisors, evaluates its curriculum, its services to children, its growth of teachers and supervisors, and its relationship to the life of the community
       d. Members of the community, especially parents, evaluate the school, its program and its teachers (The school should provide such information so as to make possible an intelligent evaluation on the community's part)
E. EVALUATION IN A UNIT OF WORK
    1. The unit should be evaluated in light of its objectives
    2. The primary objective is not absorption of a mass of facts, but the development of attitudes, understandings, and appreciations

3. The evaluation of desirable social relationships, the development of good habits of work and thought, and the imparting of basic concepts are our major social studies goals
4. Measurement of the so-called intangibles, while admittedly difficult, is possible (Formal tests, such as the California Tests of Personality and Winnetka Behavior Rating Scale are not so valuable as teacher observation and judgment)
5. The teacher, by recording objectively significant behavior, can observe the developmental pattern of growth in chidren (anecdotal records, etc.)
6. Teacher-made checklists and tests are helpful in determining growth and progress
    a. Tests in ascertaining places where information is available (A test of this type may be administered before and after a unit is taken. Growth may be measured by comparing results)
        a.1 Whom would you ask where to find a certain building if you were downtown?
        a.2 How would you locate a certain book if you were in the library?
        a.3 If you weren't sure whether a word ended in "ant" or "ent," how could you find out?
        a.4 Where would you look to find out something about an explorer?
        a.5 How could you tell, by looking at a map, whether New York is closer to Connecticut than it is to Virginia?
    b. Tests involving the relevancy of data to particular problems and tests involving the relevancy of statements to a conclusion
        b.1 Does a person's race or religion have any bearing on his athletic or musical ability?
        b.2 Since your city uses great amounts of food, does that mean that your city produces huge amounts of meat, grain, etc.?
    c. Tests involving the reliability of various sources, the matching of persons with the fields of their probable competence
        c.1 Would Mickey Mantle necessarily be an authority on international relations?
    d. Checklists of instances of voluntary cooperation (Does the child of his own accord clean up the area around his seat? Does the child bring materials from home?, etc.)
7. Methods of evaluation of a unit
    a. Objective tests *(prepared by teachers and pupils)*
    b. Teacher's written accounts and criticisms
    c. Teacher's anecdotal reports on individual and group work
    d. Matching achievement against predetermined objectives
    e. Comparison of activities and skills of this unit with those of preceding units
    f. Noting observations made by parents and community
8. Children's evaluation in a unit
    a. Charts: "Did I Do a Good Job?", etc.
    b. Evaluation "envelopes," in which children retain samples of their work and note progress
    c. Children (and teacher) appraise:
        c.1 What have we learned?
        c.2 What should we remember?
        c.3 Did we do everything we set out to do?
        c.4 What must still be done?

   c.5 What could we have done better?
   c.6 What questions should be included on a "test of all the important things we learned?"
   c.7 How can we make further use of the things we learned?
 9. Evaluation is a means of discovering:
  a. Group and individual growth
  b. Teacher-effectiveness or weakness
  c. Group needs
  d. Curriculum strengths or deficiencies
  e. Objectives realized
  f. Experience gained
  g. Subject matter acquired
  h. Skills mastered
  i. Evidences of creative expression
  j. Evidences of growth toward desirable habits, attitudes, and appreciations
  k. Activities not yet completed
  l. Subject matter not covered

V. DISCIPLINE

A. MEANING
 1. Broad Meaning - The attainment by the individual of such knowledges, skills, habits, and attitudes as will promote the well-being of himself and of his social group.
 2. Narrow Meaning - The creation of classroom conditions to provide a wholesome environment for the best functioning of the individual and the group.

B. DISCIPLINE VS. ORDER
 1. Difference
  a. Discipline: Based on self-direction; maintained by building habits of self-control and by stressing the social need for desirable conduct. It aims at a self-directed class that works quietly and efficiently even though the teacher is temporarily too busy to supervise the class.
  b. Order: Based on instant obedience to commands emanating from above; depends on the teacher's ability to exercise constant surveillance and to use the pupils' fear of detection as a deterrent to undesirable action. Order reaches its height when the teacher can make the meaningless boast that she "can hear a pin drop."
 2. As a means toward discipline, order is sometimes essential. It may be a legitimate aid to discipline. As a goal in itself, it has little justification.

C. THE DIFFERENCE BETWEEN CONDUCT AND BEHAVIOR
 1. Conduct: The adult's reaction to the child's acts. It is considered "good" or "bad." Depends on adult's standards or values.
 2. Behavior: The child's reaction to stimuli (physical, mental, or social). It is "normal" or "abnormal." Depends on child's personality.

D. PLANES OF DISCIPLINE
 1. Obedience - military concept
 2. Personal domination by the teacher - "good order" concept
 3. Social pressure - living and working with others
 4. Self-discipline - living and working alone

E. GENERAL PRINCIPLES OF CLASSROOM DISCIPLINE
   1. Self-control is achieved through proper habit formation (psychological principles)
   2. Desirable discipline is social control within the school group
   3. Discipline should be positive and constructive, rather than negative and destructive
   4. It should appeal to the highest motives of which the pupil is capable
   5. It should impress pupils as being fair, reasonable, and socially necessary
F. POSITIVE VS. NEGATIVE DISCIPLINE
   1. The essential difference is one of attitude and approach
      a. Present conformity to rule vs. cultivating motives for sound action in later years
      b. Getting children to do the right thing vs. preventing them from doing the wrong thing
   2. Examples:

   POSITIVE
   a. Stimulating attention.
   b. Creating desire to come to school because of meaningful activities.
   c. Encouraging children to come early by starting promptly with interesting work and duties.
   d. Awakening the desire to do things for the good of the school.
   e. Giving children opportunities of participating in class and school administration.

   NEGATIVE
   a. Coping with inattention. Scolding.
   b. Devising measures to curb truancy. Scolding.
   c. Devising new procedures to curb lateness. Scolding.
   d. Compelling observance of class and school rules. Punishment.
   e. Teacher does everything. Doing things for children which they can be trained to do for themselves.

   3. Caution: It is impossible to dispense with negative discipline entirely, but the emphasis should be placed on the positive plane.
G. WHY SOME TEACHERS HAVE DISCIPLINARY TROUBLES
   1. Pedagogical Reasons
      a. Failure to employ appropriate subject matter and materials
      b. Poor teaching techniques
      c. Failure to consider the individual pupil's capacities, talents, and interests
   2. Classroom Management
      a. Failure to mechanize routines
      b. Unattractive, physically uncomfortable surroundings
   3. Personality
      a. Lack of tact
      b. High strung manner
      c. Idiosyncrasies in dress
      d. High pitched voice
      e. Lack of a sense of humor
   4. Psychological
      a. Lack of sympathy with children
      b. Procrastination in handling cases (not facing the issue)
      c. Lack of a fair disciplinary policy
H. CLASS MORALE AS A FACTOR IN CLASSROOM DISCIPLINE
   1. Meaning of morale or class spirit

      a. "Morale is the feeling among members of a group that stimulates them to work happily together toward the realization of shared aims"
      b. "The personality of the group born of common attitudes"
  2. How Developed
    L a. *Leadership* of the teacher - she sets the tone
        a.1 Her personality - ability to fire others with enthusiasm for ideals and service; to arouse faith of pupils in her
        a.2 Her educational qualifications
        a.3 Her understanding of children
    A b. Stressing of strong social *attitudes* - work of the group more important than that of the individual - team work of pupils
    C c. Situations arousing *common* loyalties - participation in joint efforts
        c.1 Class projects - making things for the class or the school (posters, art objects, Christmas gifts to soldiers or destitute children, class newspaper, class party, help with parents' bazaar)
        c.2 Assembly programs, pageants
        c.3 Athletic teams
        c.4 Friendly competition with other classes (attendance records, contributions to the Red Cross)
    P d. Situations arousing *pride* as a result of achievement and recognition
        d.1 Service to the class and school
        d.2 Records - attendance, punctuality, neatness, cleanliness, etc.
        d.3 Good deeds and accomplishments of classmates
        d.4 Accomplishment of learning goals (New Program)
    S e. Attractive surroundings - contribution of pupils to the appearance of the room
                  (*Mnemonic* - *S C A L P)*

I. THE USE OF INCENTIVES
  1. Distinction between incentives and motives
    a. Incentive - An environmental object or condition, the attainment or avoidance of which motivates behavior (external) - praise, blame, reward, punishment, rivalry
    b. Motive - The process within an organism which energizes or directs it toward a specific line of behavior (internal) - interest, need, urge, drive, desire
    c. Incentive is the stimulus; motive is the reaction, though the terms, including "motivation," are used loosely and interchangeably.
  2. Real vs. Artificial Motivation (intrinsic vs. extrinsic)
    a. Real Motivation - Gives purpose and direction to the learning process, is part of the task, arises from the value of the task for its own sake, is related to the life of the child (aroused by problems or challenges to which the child desires the answer or solution)
    b. Artificial Motivation - attempts to make uninteresting material attractive by sugarcoating; is based on traditional attitude that every lesson is a unit in itself; is usually unrelated or only slightly related to the task (stores, games, marks, rewards)

c. The new program vs. the traditional program from the point of view of motivation
   d. Some examples of real and artificial motivation:

REAL	ARTIFICIAL
1. Arithmetic: Learning percents through computing class averages in attendance or the standing of athletic teams	1. Learning by reference to father's bank account
2. Spelling: Learning words by writing a real letter	2. Learning through the desire to get a better mark
3. Geography: Learning the geography of the city through trips and excursions	3. Learning in order to do well on a quiz
4. Science: Learning about plants through growing them	4. Learning through a reference to the flower shop around the corner or to a picture
5. Social Studies: Learning the industries of a country through a study of how people live and work	5. Learning through reference to the work children's parents do
6. Art: Learning color and perspective through illustrating a unit by murals	6. Learning in order to get a good mark, to have work displayed, or to obtain the approval of the teacher

   (NOTE: *Extrinsic motivation is sometimes justifiable or desirable, but it should be subordinated to intrinsic drives wherever possible.*)
3. Incentives in the Classroom
   a. Principles
      a.1 The best incentive is one which makes a task significant to the child
      a.2 It should influence future as well as present actions and attitudes
      a.3 It should make doing an act a satisfying process
      a.4 It should encourage the social point of view
   b. Motives to which the teacher can appeal
      b.1 The desire to do the right for its own sake should always be the ultimate goal even with very young children
      b.2 The desire for self-respect - knowledge of progress, recognition of abilities or status
      b.3 The desire to win the approval of one's fellow - displaying good work, posting lists of children doing well, monitorships
      b.4 The desire to gain the approval of the teacher or one's parents - praise succeeds better than blame, recognizing the good better than scolding the bad, letters to parents
      b.5 The desire for new experiences - problems, excursions, class clubs, projects
      b.6 The desire to win a reward - need not be of material value - praise, exhibition of work, monitorships should be within reach of all - avoid bribery
   (NOTE: *The lowest form of incentive is better than the best form of punishment.*)
J. CLASSROOM PUNISHMENTS
   1. The Basis for Punishment
      a. What should be the aim? Retributive, deterrent, or corrective?
      b. Punishment may be justified if it is *corrective*
         b.1 It must be a means of removing a tendency to unsocial behavior

    b.2 It must not be a separate entity, but part of the education process
    b.3 It must aid in the process of adjusting behavior in a positive direction
   c. Criteria of effective punishment
    c.1 The child should be shown that he is being punished for a social transgression
    c.2 The teacher's personal feelings must not be a consideration
    c.3 Punishment is to be used only when the child fails to respond to incentives
    c.4 It should be adapted to the child (not uniform)
    c.5 It must not be unduly severe
    c.6 It must not leave a residue of antagonism or resentment
    c.7 It must not constitute the complete treatment for problem behavior
2. Punishment by Natural Consequence
  a. It is sound in theory but difficult in practice in the classroom (copying, cheating, failing to do work, obscene language)
  b. The principle can be followed, by making punishment seem to be a natural consequence wherever possible
3. Punishment by Fear
  a. Fear is an inhibiting rather than a stimulating force. It has a paralyzing harmful effect on development. It should rarely be used
  b. Corporal punishment is the lowest form of the use of fear. If ever administered, it should be for its shocking effect, rather than for punitive or corrective reasons
4. Evaluation of Classroom Punishments
  a. Minor punishments, such as staring at a child or calling his name - effective in nipping trouble in the bud
  b. Deprivation of position - effective if the door is held open for reinstatement
  c. Reprimands - effective, if given unemotionally and child is shown how his act interferes with others (must be used sparingly)
  d. Doing a written task - ineffective because it avoids the true causes of the trouble (I must come to school on time) and builds wrong associations (writing spelling words twenty five times)
  e. Picking up papers, etc. - effective if used as a means of making up for an offense, doing a positive deed in place of a negative
  f. Detention - generally ineffective because it leads to wrong associations with school
  g. Isolation - of doubtful value. The practice of having a child stand in a corner or in the corridor has no justification
  h. Social disapproval - effective if public humiliation does not result
  i. Saturation - ineffective and dangerous (it may backfire)
  j. Sarcasm - dangerous because mistaken for humor, builds resentment instead of cooperation (of doubtful value even with "smart alecks")
  k. Epithets - unjustified
  l. Sending for parent - effective if designed to understand causes and to devise program for cooperation between home and school

K. SOME PRACTICAL SUGGESTIONS FOR TEACHERS *(CHARACTERISTIC OF TRANSITION FROM ORDER TO DISCIPLINE)*
   1. Give pupils the impression that you expect perfect order
   2. Learn the names of all pupils as soon as possible
   3. Give no unnecessary orders or directions - no repetitions
   4. An explanatory statement, preparatory to giving a direction or order, reduces the possibility of confusion or disobedience
   5. Insist upon a reasonable compliance with those directions which are given
   6. Don't let little things go *(Nip disorder in the bud)*
   7. Keep the machinery of class management simple
   8. Plan lessons and all work well
   9. Keep the class busy on worthwhile work and activities
   10. Use rewards and punishments judiciously - watch for and reward desirable actions
   11. Avoid punishing in anger (It's the child, not the offense, that must be considered)
   12. Don't punish the group for the offense of an individual
   13. Don't make threats
   14. Severe penalties should not be used for minor offenses
   15. The teacher should never give the impression that she has exhausted her supply of punishments or rewards
   16. Avoid forcing an issue with a disobedient pupil before the class
   17. When a child is punished, keep the door open for him to return to the good graces of the class and the teacher
   18. Have a sense of humor
   19. Be fair and consistent in your decisions
   20. Have an element of surprise - something new - in class work
   21. Seat pupils so that opportunities for infraction are lessened
   22. The voice should be subdued, but audible enough to be heard clearly throughout the room
   23. Primarily, the handling of discipline cases is the responsibility of the teacher
   24. In handling discipline cases, the teacher may have reasonable recourse to the parents
   25. When a teacher has exhausted her own resources, or in the cases of emergency, she should call upon the supervisor for help

VI. BASIC FUNDAMENTALS OF EDUCATIONAL PSYCHOLOGY

A. CONDITIONING
   Learning takes place as a result of experience with outside stimuli. Responses are established by means of fixed associations.
   1. Principles of Conditioning *(for use by teachers)*
      a. Learners' responses must be systematically studied
      b. Records of progress indicate need for change of pace, concentration on difficult parts, return to basic skills, new motivation, variations in use of cues
      c. Learner should make own records of progress
      d. Unlearning takes place rapidly; support and repeated reinforcement are required to consolidate and maintain habitual performance
      e. Teacher must control stimulating conditions (motivation)
      f. Teacher must help learner by providing varying conditions and extended practice
      g. Forced pacing methods are a poor substitute for adequate motivation

B. LEARNING BY TRIAL AND ERROR (CONNECTIONISM)
   Learning involves the making of new mental and neural connections and the discarding or strengthening of old connections.
   1. Concerned with what takes place between S-R to the neural connections
      a. Atomistic analysis of behavior
      b. Development is from hereditary instincts and reflexes to acquired habits
      c. Intellect and intelligence are quantitative
   2. Thorndike's Laws of Learning
      a. Readiness - When a conduction unit is ready to act, conduction by it is satisfying and failure to conduct or being forced when not ready is annoying.
      b. Exercise - (Use and Disuse) Repetition with satisfaction strengthens the connection; disuse weakens the connection.
      c. Effect - Satisfaction strengthens the connection which it follows and to which it belongs. *(Importance of motivation)*
   3. Thorndike's Five Characteristics of Learning
      a. Multiple responses to the same external situation pervade nine tenths of learning.
      b. The responses made are the product of the "set" or "attitude" of the learner. The satisfaction or annoyance produced by a response is conditioned by the learner's attitude.
      c. Partial Activity: One or another element in the situation may be prepotent in determining the response.
      d. Law of Assimilation or Analogy: If one element in the situation resembles another, it will call forth a corresponding response.
      e. Associative Shifting - Omitting elements of a situation and still getting the same response. *(Conditioned response)*
   4. The Significance of "Cues" in Learning
      a. The learner tends to respond to loud sound, intense, brilliant or rapidly changing cues.
      b. Conspicuous stimuli may receive undue attention. Important stimuli may thus be overlooked.
      c. Cues help emphasize important stimuli.
      d. The teacher must discover when to use proper cues, and how much guidance to give the learner.
C. LEARNING BY INSIGHT: GESTALT PSYCHOLOGY
   1. Constant striving to make sense out of a situation
   2. The learner's efforts are not purely random
   3. Understanding is enhanced by responding to total patterns, to relation between things
   4. Motivation helps create perception of the problem
   5. The learner's background of experience aids in insight, in perceiving figurations, in seeing the relationships of the parts to the whole, and in acquiring meaning and value
D. THE FIELD THEORY (ORGANISMIC, HOLISTIC THEORY)
   1. Derived from the Gestalt theory
   2. Insight is the alteration of organic structure within an area of the "whole organism"
   3. Significances
      a. Breakdown of atomistic views
      b. Importance of chemical function of neural mechanisms
      c. Fundamental role of "feelings and emotions" in learning

d. Muscular coordination of the complete organism is a factor in skill acquisition
   e. Recognition of the principle of maturation
   f. Best motivation derives from needs of learners
E. TRANSFER OF TRAINING
   1. Recognized as significant in educational theory and practice
      a. Traditional Concept - Doctrine of Formal Discipline: the mind gains strength through use, and this strength is automatically available in all situations. (Faculties of the Mind)
      b. Current Concept - No faculties as such. Transfer is a fact of mental life occurring under certain mental conditions, not because of external causes.
   2. Factors Influencing Transfer
      a. Methods of procedure in learning and teaching
      b. Attitude of readiness set up by instructions given
      c. Degree of mastery of the material learned
      d. Integration of the initial learning - as to content and method
      e. Extent to which generalization and application are applied - "psychological organization"
   3. Current Theories of Transfer
      a. Theory of Identical Elements (Thorndike)
         a.1 Identity of content
         a.2 Identity of procedure
         a.3 Identity of aims or ideals
         These identical elements make use of the same neural bonds.
      b. Theory of Generalization or Abstraction or Relationship
         Transfer takes place to the extent that one generalizes his experiences and is able to apply general principles to different situations. (Scientific method)
   4. Implications for the Supervisor
      a. Materials used should have real value for children, not for mental discipline.
      b. A subject which has slight transfer value in a large field may be of more value than a subject which has a greater transfer value, but in a very limited field.
      c. The difficulty of a subject is not any indication of its transfer value.
      d. Recognition of child growth and development is the basic aim.
      e. The position accorded any subject in the school curriculum should be decided by the value of the special training it affords and by the social significance of its content rather than by its promise to develop general intellectual capacities.
   5. Implications for the Teacher
      a. The most effective use of knowledge is assured, not through acquisition of any particular item of experience but only through the establishment of associations which give it general value.
      b. Transfer is most common at the higher levels of intellectual activity.
      c. Children should receive training in methods of memorizing, acquiring skills, and in solving problems.
      d. If transfer value is slight, then it is most economical to practice directly those habits and skills we wish to develop.
      e. An individual's ability to apply knowledge is not in proportion to his knowledge of facts.

    f. The teacher should know what it is that she wants the children to transfer to other fields, and she must learn by experience or experiment how to teach for transfer.
    g. The theory of transfer is recognized by all schools of psychology. More research is necessary before teachers can be guided by the theory to any great extent.

F. HABIT
1. Meaning - A learned response made automatically to the appropriate stimulus.
2. Principles of Habit Formation (Bagley)
    a. Focalize consciousness (Motivation)
        a.1 Give clearest possible idea of habit to be formed
        a.2 Use demonstration   a.3 Make it vivid
        a.4 Arouse motivation
        a.5 Give instruction in how habits are formed
        a.6 Multiple sense appeal
    b. Attentive repetition
        b.1 Vigorous, short, definite drill   b.2 Use devices
        b.3 Have a definite goal (focalization)
        b.4 Watch for lag in attention
        b.5 Vary the number of repetitions
        b.6 "Practice makes perfect" only if with attention
    c. No exceptions
        c.1 Analyze habit in advance to prepare for likely slips
        c.2 Give special drill on difficult parts
        c.3 Put child on his guard   c.4 Remove opposing stimuli
        c.5 Avoid forming similar habits at the same time
        c.6 Punishment, if necessary, should follow wrong act
    d. Automatization
        d.1 Attention to weak elements
        d.2 Distribution of practice (optional length)
3. Values and Limitations
    a. Diminishes fatigue because habit mechanizes reactions so that they accomplish their function with directness and minimum time and effort
    b. Releases consciousness for the guidance of other activities
    c. Makes responses reliable and accurate
    d. Complete domination, however, retards progress
    e. Sensibilities often deadened, lessening normal emotional tones
    f. Difficult to break bad habits
4. Breaking Bad Habits
    a. Avoid the situation which will result in the undesirable habit
    b. Avoid opportunity for its practice
    c. Concentrate on one or two bad habits at a time
    d. Follow the principles of habit formation for developing the reverse of the bad habit (Substitution)
    e. Attach unpleasant feeling tone
5. Significance for Teaching
    a. Dependence of habit on sensory stimulation *(Habits never initiate themselves)*
    b. Importance of gradation of subject matter to develop mechanical habits
    c. In skills, improvement is very rapid at first
    d. Attention to physical and psychical conditions (time of day, length of period, etc.)

  e. Recognition of possible periods of lapse and plateau
    e. 1 Need for rest
    e. 2 Attention and interest misdirected
    e. 3 Conflict in habits
    e. 4 Minor causes - indisposition, irritation
  f. Recognition of individual differences in habit formation
  g. Rate of forgetting high at first
  h. Consideration of Speed vs. Accuracy
  i. Recognition of three sets of habits (Mechanical; Subject Matter; Mental)

G. INDIVIDUAL DIFFERENCES
 1. Principles
  a. Pupils differ in degree of ability, not in the ability itself
  b. Individuals differ in degree of difficulty of tasks which they can learn; also in the method of learning
  c. Pupils of the same age and grade differ greatly - there is considerable overlapping of successive grades
  d. No one class can ever be entirely homogeneous - variations are continuous
  e. There are no readily available and fixed categories which the school can employ for the purpose of differentiated instruction
  f. Provision for individualization presents teaching and **administrative** difficulties
  g. Chronological age alone cannot be the determinant of an individual's capacity
 2. Conclusions for the School
  a. Administrative
    a. 1 Vary the time element
    a. 2 Flexible grouping
    a. 3 Testing programs
    a. 4 Modification of the curriculum
    a. 5 Provision for educational guidance
    a. 6 Flexible promotions
    a. 7 Supervision of proper teaching practices
  b. Curricular
    b. 1 Individualization of instruction
    b. 2 Diagnostic testing and remedial teaching
    b. 3 Provision for individual methods of learning
    b. 4 Grouping within the class
    b. 5 Record of needs, progress, and evaluation

VII. HISTORY OF EDUCATION

A. LEADERS
 1. Socrates (5th century B.C.)(469-399 B.C.)(Athens, Period of Sophists)
  (1) Writings - Left no writings, is studied in works of Plato and Xenophon.
  (2) Emphasis - Highest formulation of principles of moral life up to his time.
  (3) Contributions - His starting point: "Man is the measure of all things" (Protagoras).
  (4) Developed opinion into true or universal knowledge.
  (5) Aid of education: Not sophist brilliancy of speech, but knowledge arising from power of thought, analysis of experience.
  (6) Method: Dialectic, skillful questioning, distinguishing between permanent form and changing appearance, forming concepts from percepts.

2. Plato (4th century B.C.) (429-348 B.C.) (Athens, Academy)
   (1) Writings - "Republic," "Dialogues."
   (2) Three social classes: philosophers, warriors, workers.
   (3) Six major concerns of life: psychology, knowledge, soul, state, politics, ethics.
   (4) The ideal *State*, which exists for the realization of *justice*, consists of three classes of people: philosophers, soldiers, and workers.
   These classes of society correspond to the soul (or *psychology*) of the individual: intelligence or reason; the passions, spirit or will; and the desires, appetites, or sensations.
   The *ethics* of the classes embraces the traits of character which they should exhibit: wisdom, or correctness of thought; honor, courage, energy of will, or justice of the heart; and temperance, self-control, or justice of the senses.
   Politics indicates the duties of the classes: the philosophers are to rule, the soldiers to protect and defend the State, and the workers to obey and support those above them.
   (5) Aim of education: To discover and develop individual qualifications to fit into classes of society; harmony of individual and social motives.
3. Aristotle (3rd century B.C.) (384-322 B.C.)(Athens, Lyceum)
   (1) Writings - "Organon," "Politics," "Ethics," "Metaphysics."
   (2) Like Plato, he believed the highest art of man to be to direct society so as to produce the greatest good for mankind.
   (3) Education is subject to politics, each kind of state having its appropriate kind of education.
   (4) Education is a life activity.
   (5) Method: Objective and scientific; used inductive method, and thus founded practically all the modern sciences.
   (6) Education democratic, although all could not reach the same high point.
   (7) Greatest systematizer of knowledge.
   (8) Formulated deductive reasoning; dialectic given form and universal influence.
   (9) Gave vocabulary of reasoning to the world.
4. Comenius (17th century) (1592-1670)
   (1) Writings - "Orbus Pictus," "Vestibulum,""Janua,""School of Infancy," "The Great Didactic"
   (2) Sense - realist
      a. The teacher should appeal through sense-perception to understand the child
   (3) Contributions
      a. Forerunner of 18th and 19th century educational theory
      b. Reformed Latin textbooks
5. John Locke (17th century) (1632-1704)
   (1) Writings - "Essay on Conduct of the Human Understanding," "Thoughts"
   (2) Founder of modern psychology; advocate of faculty psychology
   (3) Empiricism; induction
   (4) Conception of the child's mind as a "tabula rasa" (blank slate)
   (5) His influence strong up to the middle of the 19th century
6. Rousseau (18th century) (1712-1778)
   (1) Writings - "La Nouvelle Heloise," "Emile"
   (2) Education is life, not preparation for life
   (3) Importance of the child
   (4) Functional education
   (5) Individual differences

7. Johann Bernard Basedow (18th century)(1723-1790)
    (1) Writings -"Elementarwerk," "Book of Method"; established school called Philanthropinum, at Dessau.
    (2) Belongs to the line of Sense-Realists following Rousseau and forerunner to Pestalozzi.
    (3) Made first attempt since Comeniums to improve the work of the school through the use of appropriate textbooks.
    (4) Ideas embodied:
        (a) Children to be treated as such, not as adults.
        (b) Each child taught a handicraft for educational and social reasons.
        (c) Vernacular rather than classical languages chief subject matter of education.
        (d) Instruction connected with realities rather than with words.
        (e) Rich and poor educated together.
    (5) Contributions
        (a) Trained teachers.
        (b) Milder form of discipline.
        (c) Broader and more philanthropic view of man's duty to his fellow-man.
8. Pestalozzi (18th and early 19th century)(1746-1827)
    (1) Writings - "How Gertrude Teaches Her Children," "Leonard and Gertrude"
    (2) Sense impression
    (3) Respect for the individuality of the child
    (4) Discipline based upon love
    (5) Education for the subnormal
    (6) Normal schools
9. Herbart (19th and first half of the 19th century)(1776-1841)
    (1) Writings - First to write a textbook on psychology,"Testbook of Psychology"; Psychology as a Science"
    (2) Rejected the faculty psychology of Pestalozzi
    (3) Substituted his own method - the Five Formal Steps:
        (a) Preparation   (b) Presentation   (c) Comparison
        (d) Generalization (e) Application
    (4) Organization and technique of classroom instruction
    (5) Emphasis on environment in education
10. Froebel (first half of 19th century)(1782-1852)
    (1) Writings - "Education of Man," "Mutter," "Kose Lieder"
    (2) Founder of the kindergarten and the kindergarten idea
    (3) Education by doing
11. Spencer, Herbert (19th century) (1820-1903)
    (1) Writings - "Principles of Psychology," "Synthetic Philosophy," "Essays on Education"
    (2) Not originator but developer of the best in democratic education of his predecessors
    (3) Emphasis on scientific knowledge
12. Mann, Horace (19th century) (1796-1859)
    (1) Reference: Mary T.Mann, ed.,"The Life and Works of Horace Mann" (5 vols.-1891)
    (2) First secretary of the first Board of Education of Massachusetts (1817)
    (3) Conception of education as universal, secular, public, free, and compulsory
    (4) Outstanding organizer in education

13. Barnard, Henry (19th century) (1811-1900)
    (1) Writings - Edited "The American Journal of Education"(1855-187
    (2) Held positions in Connecticut and Rhode Island similar to that of Horace Mann in Massachusetts, i.e., Secretary of the Board of Education in Connecticut, 1838-1842, 1851-1855; and State Superintendent of Education in Rhode Island, 1845-1849.
    (3) First United States Commissioner of Education 1867-1870
14. Dewey, John (19th and 20th century) (1859-1952)
    (1) Writings - "The School and Society,""Democracy and Education," "Experience and Nature," "Freedom and Culture"
    (2) Education is life, not a preparation for life
    (3) Learning takes place by doing
    (4) The bases of education are psychological and sociological
    (5) Father of progressive education ("activity" program)

B. CONCEPTUALIZED DEFINITIONS AND AIMS OF EDUCATION
    1. Character, morality: Plutarch (Spartans), Herbart
    2. Perfect development: Plato, Rabelais, Montaigne, Comenius, Locke, Parker, Pestalozzi
    3. Happiness: Aristotle, James Mill
    4. Truth: Socrates
    5. Citizenship: Luther, Milton
    6. Mastery of nature: Bacon, Huxley
    7. Religion: Comenius
    8. Mental power, discipline: Locke, Van Dyke, Ruediger
    9. Preparation for the future: Kant
    10. Habits: Rousseau, William James
    11. Unfolding: Froebel, Hegel
    12. Holy life: Froebel
    13. Interests: Herbart
    14. Knowledge: L.F. Ward
    15. Complete living: Spencer
    16. Culture, liberal education: Dewey
    17. Skill: Nathaniel Butler, E.C. Moore
    18. Inheritance of culture: N.M. Butler
    19. Socialization: W.T. Harris, Dewey
    20. Social efficiency: Dewey, Bagley
    21. Adjustment: Dewey, Ruediger, Chapman and Counts
    22. Growth: Dewey
    23. Organization of experience: Dewey
    24. Self realization: Dewey and Tufts
    25. Satisfying wants: Thorndike and Gates
    26. Insight: Gentile

ANSWER SHEET

TEST NO. _____ PART _____ TITLE OF POSITION _____
(AS GIVEN IN EXAMINATION ANNOUNCEMENT - INCLUDE OPTION, IF ANY)

PLACE OF EXAMINATION _____ (CITY OR TOWN) _____ (STATE) _____ DATE _____

RATING

USE THE SPECIAL PENCIL. MAKE GLOSSY BLACK MARKS.

Make only ONE mark for each answer. Additional and stray marks may be counted as mistakes. In making corrections, erase errors COMPLETELY.

ANSWER SHEET

TEST NO. _____ PART _____ TITLE OF POSITION _____
(AS GIVEN IN EXAMINATION ANNOUNCEMENT - INCLUDE OPTION, IF ANY)

PLACE OF EXAMINATION _____ (CITY OR TOWN) _____ (STATE) _____ DATE _____

RATING

USE THE SPECIAL PENCIL. MAKE GLOSSY BLACK MARKS.

Make only ONE mark for each answer. Additional and stray marks may be counted as mistakes. In making corrections, erase errors COMPLETELY.

9392

REF
LB
2844.1
.A8   This is your
N31   passbook for
       teachers license
       examinations :
       auxiliary teacher

DATE			
	REFERENCE		

FORM 125 M

Cop. 1

SOCIAL SCIENCES & HISTORY DIVISION

The Chicago Public Library

Received OCT 2 2 1979

© THE BAKER & TAYLOR CO.